W9-AWF-196

Language Handbook

Grade 3

Requests for permission to make copies of any part of the work should be mailed to: Permissions Department, Harcourt Brace & Company, 6277 Sea Harbor Drive, Orlando, Florida 32887-6777.

Printed in the United States of America

ISBN 0-15-304867-0

13 073 98

HARCOURT BRACE & COMPANY

ORLANDO · ATLANTA · AUSTIN · BOSTON · SAN FRANCISCO · CHICAGO · DALLAS · NEW YORK · TORONTO · LONDON

WRITING FORMS

GRAMMAR, USAGE, AND MECHANICS

GRAMMAR

HANDWRITING

ADDITIONAL PRACTICE

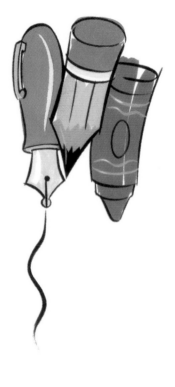

What's the first thing you do when you get a new magazine or book? You look through it to see what is inside. Take a minute to look through the pages of this handbook to see what's inside.

WHAT IS A HANDBOOK?

A handbook is like a toolbox. It holds all the tools you need to do different tasks. In this handbook, the tools are language.

Use this language handbook as a guide to all kinds of helpful tips for writing, speaking, and listening. You will find

- ☑ tips to help you start writing.
- ☑ information about writing forms.
- ☑ handwriting models and hints.
- ☑ easy-to-understand rules of grammar.
- ☑ practice with language.

Think of this handbook as a toolbox full of language tools.

SECTIONS OF THE HANDBOOK

This handbook has five sections. Four of the sections include information about writing, writing forms, grammar, and handwriting. The fifth section provides practice with language.

Use the sections of this book to find tools to help you read, write, speak, and listen.

WRITING

This section includes all the information you need to plan, write, and polish your writing.

WRITING FORMS

This section shows models for writing stories, poems, how-to paragraphs — and more.

GRAMMAR, USAGE, AND MECHANICS

In this section, you will find information about parts of speech, sentences, and punctuation.

HANDWRITING

This section gives suggestions for making your handwriting clear for your readers.

ADDITIONAL PRACTICE

Exercises in this section help you practice the rules of grammar, usage, and mechanics.

HOW TO FIND INFORMATION IN THE HANDBOOK

Use this handbook as a reference tool to help you find the answers to your questions about language. Two of the best ways to find information in this book are to use the table of contents and the index.

- The **table of contents** follows the title page, or first page, of this book. It tells you the main sections of this book. It also tells you the page on which each section begins. Use the table of contents when you want to find main topics quickly.

- The **index** is at the back of the book. It lists every topic in this book. It also tells the pages on which the information appears. Topics are listed in alphabetical order so that you can find them quickly.

BONUS

Each section begins with a short table of contents. The first one is on the next page.

Writing

The Writing Process

When you write, it helps if you have a plan. The writing process is a plan that helps you organize your thoughts and write about them. The writing process is divided into five steps.

PREWRITING

Identify your TAP—task, audience, and purpose. Then choose your topic. Gather information about your topic, and then organize it.

DRAFTING

Put your ideas in writing. Don't worry about mistakes. You can fix them later.

RESPONDING AND REVISING

Read over what you've written. Does it fit your purpose? Talk about your writing with a partner or in a group. Revise it to make it better.

PROOFREADING

Fix errors in spelling, grammar, and word use. Check punctuation. Also, check that you have used capital letters correctly.

PUBLISHING

Share your writing with others. There are many ways to publish your work!

You can move back and forth between the steps of the writing process.

Planning Tips

Writing begins as soon as you begin thinking about what to write. Use these ideas to help you plan your writing.

Writing is a snap when you know your TAP.

UNDERSTANDING TASK, AUDIENCE, AND PURPOSE

Before you begin writing, know your TAP— your task, audience, and purpose. Ask yourself these questions:

Task

- **What am I going to write?**

  Will I write a story, a letter, or something else?

Audience

- **Who will read this?**

  Am I writing to a friend or a teacher, or for myself or someone else?

Purpose

- **Why am I writing?**

  Am I giving information, telling a story, or writing for another reason?

GATHERING INFORMATION

Are there times you feel stuck or don't know what to write about? Here are some things you can do to get ideas for writing.

- Look in your journal or portfolio.

- Make a list.

- Brainstorm with a group or a friend.

- Freewrite. (This means just start writing and don't stop.)

- Ask *Who? What? When? Where? Why? How?*

- Read a magazine or a book to get ideas.

- Use graphic organizers.

Make a chart or a web to help you find ideas.

FIRST DAY OF SCHOOL

nice teacher

new friends

homework

loud bells

new friends

homework

nice teacher

loud bells

FIRST DAY OF SCHOOL

An **inverted triangle** is another useful graphic organizer. Use it to narrow a topic. Write a topic in the top part. Write a smaller topic in the next part. Write an example in the bottom part. This is the topic you write about.

Use graphic organizers to find ideas for writing.

Pets that work

Guide dogs

German shepherds

Use a **star** graphic organizer when you are writing to describe something. Write your topic in the center. On each point, write words that tell how your topic looks, feels, sounds, smells, and tastes.

Look green

Taste sour

Feel wet and slimy

Dill Pickles

Smell spicy

Sound crunchy

ORGANIZING WRITING

After you have gathered ideas and information, you can begin to organize them.

A **story map** helps you plan a story. It gets you to think about the title, the setting, the characters, the problem, and the solution.

Graphic organizers also help you organize ideas and information.

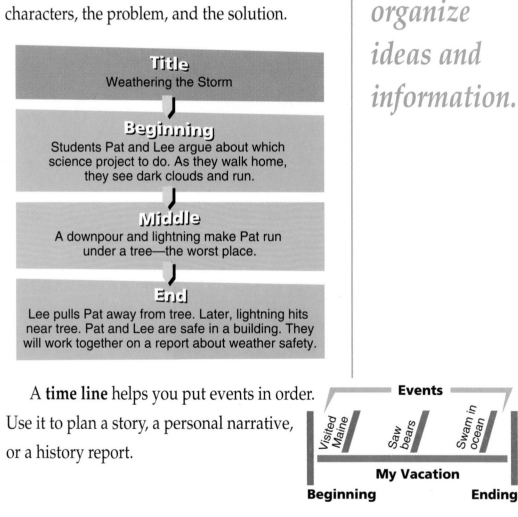

Title
Weathering the Storm

Beginning
Students Pat and Lee argue about which science project to do. As they walk home, they see dark clouds and run.

Middle
A downpour and lightning make Pat run under a tree—the worst place.

End
Lee pulls Pat away from tree. Later, lightning hits near tree. Pat and Lee are safe in a building. They will work together on a report about weather safety.

A **time line** helps you put events in order. Use it to plan a story, a personal narrative, or a history report.

Events

Visited Maine

Saw bears

Swam in ocean

My Vacation

Beginning

Ending

Use a **Venn diagram** when you want to write a paragraph about how people, places, or things are the same or different.

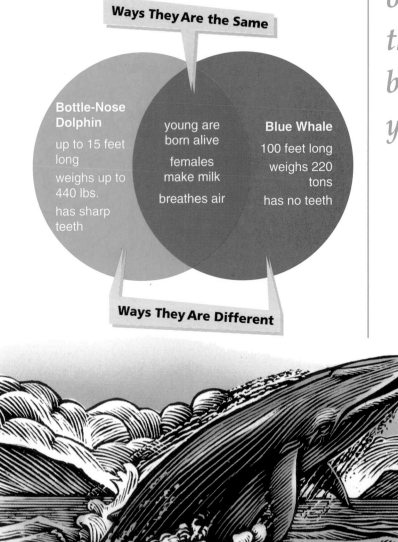

Ways They Are the Same

Bottle-Nose Dolphin

up to 15 feet long

weighs up to 440 lbs.

has sharp teeth

young are born alive

females make milk

breathes air

Blue Whale

100 feet long

weighs 220 tons

has no teeth

Ways They Are Different

Choose the graphic organizer that works best for your TAP.

A **how-to chart** helps you put in order the steps for directions or a how-to paragraph. First, write the materials needed. Then list the steps in order.

How to Make a Paper Quilt	
Materials:	colored paper, pencil and pad, paste, scissors, poster board
Step 1	Sketch a favorite pattern or family design 4 times.
Step 2	Cut different colors of paper and paste on sketches.
Step 3	Paste the four sketches onto poster board.
Step 4	Sign and present to family.

An **outline** also helps you put information in order. Use an outline to organize notes for a research report.

Topic: Raccoons
I. Main Idea: Northern raccoons
A. Detail: Live in North and Central America
B. Detail: Have thick, long gray fur
C. Detail: Eat crab, fish, acorns, nuts
II. Main Idea: Crab-eating raccoons
A. Detail: Live in Central and South America
B. Detail: Have short, thin fur
C. Detail: Eat same food as northern raccoons

Writing Tips

Even when you have a topic and a plan, you may find it hard to begin writing. Don't worry! Here are some ideas to help you.

GETTING STARTED

If you can't seem to find the right way to begin your writing, don't start at the beginning. Start in the middle or even at the end! You can go back later and add the beginning. Use these tips to get started.

- Relax. Pretend you're writing to a friend.
- Change how you write. Instead of writing by hand, use a computer.
- Draw a picture. Then write about it.
- Imagine yourself writing.
- Freewrite until you feel comfortable.
- Use your notes.

Start writing the way that feels best for you.

WRITING A GOOD BEGINNING

A good beginning in a paragraph or a report should be interesting. It should also tell readers what your writing is about. Remember to state your topic clearly.

KEEPING YOUR AUDIENCE'S ATTENTION

Once you have stated your topic, you want to keep your audience's attention. Here are some tips for keeping your audience interested.

- **Use vivid words.**
- **Tell interesting or unusual facts.**
- **Give specific examples.**

Grab your readers' attention at the beginning. Keep it until the end!

21

Polishing Your Writing

When you polish your writing, you **revise,** or change, parts of it to make it better. Here are some things you can do to polish your work.

- **Add** words, sentences, or paragraphs.

- **Cut** information that you don't need.

- **Replace** information with new or better information.

- **Move** information around so that it's in an order that makes sense.

REVISING CONFERENCES

One way to improve your writing is to get someone else's opinion about it. Work with one or more partners to help you revise your writing. Use these tips to help you.

- Be positive and polite.

- Ask questions rather than criticize.

- Work together to get the best results.

Editor's Marks

∧   **Add something.**

  Cut something.

  Replace something.

  Move something.

Revising Checklist

☑ **Does my topic sentence tell the main idea?**

☑ **Do my detail sentences support my topic sentence?**

☑ **Have I grouped or ordered information in a way that makes sense?**

☑ **Are my sentences clear? Have I avoided run-on sentences?**

RESPONDING AND REVISING STRATEGIES

EXPANDING YOUR WRITING

You can make your writing more interesting by expanding and combining sentences. Expand sentences by adding details that create a vivid word picture.

Lee ran_∧ nervously into the yard.

Combining short, choppy sentences makes your writing flow more smoothly.

Same Subject

Tina saw the puppy_∧ ~~Tina~~ ran to it.
(and)

Same Predicate

Tina_∧ ~~was ready.~~ Lee was ready.
(and) *(were)*

Two Sentences

Tricky barked_∧ ~~Then~~ she sat up.
(and)

Use a comma before *and* when you join two sentences.

The word and is often used to combine sentence parts.

USING FIGURATIVE LANGUAGE

Paint vivid word pictures for your readers. One way to do this is to compare things that are both different and alike in some way.

Compare to help your readers see things in new ways.

Using as *and* like *to compare*

You can compare by using the words *as* or *like*.

The dog was <u>as</u> slippery <u>as</u> an eel.
The dog was <u>like</u> a slippery eel.

Complete these sentences so that your readers "see" something in a new way.

The dog's fur was as _____ as _____.

The dog's fur was like _____.

Using is *to compare*

You can also compare things by saying that one thing *is* another.

The garden <u>is</u> a treasure chest.

EDITING WORDY SENTENCES

When you polish your writing, you may find that more isn't always better. Say what you mean in as few words as you need to use.

grabbed
Lee ~~made a grab~~ for Tricky, ~~who~~
~~was slippery,~~ but the dog's muddy
fur made her hard to hold.

The words *made a grab for* were replaced with one word, *grabbed*. The words *who was slippery* were cut because they did not add meaning.

USING VIVID WORDS

Use a dictionary or a thesaurus to replace an unclear or overused word with one that says exactly what you mean. Exact nouns and verbs will help to make your sentences exciting.

puppy scampered   rosebush
The ~~dog ran~~ under a ~~bush.~~

Choose vivid words to make your writing sparkle.

Polishing Your Writing

P R O O F R E A D I N G   T I P S

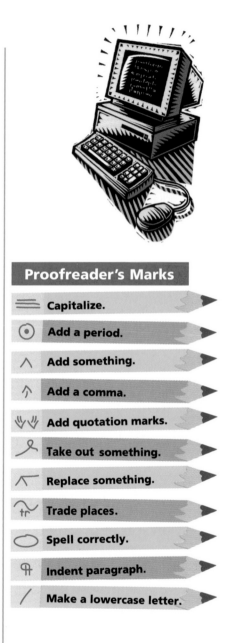

You've revised your writing, but you're not ready to publish it until you proofread it. Proofreading means checking for errors in spelling, grammar, and word use. Here are some tips to help you proofread in different ways.

- Use a dictionary to check spelling.
- Read your writing aloud to find mistakes, such as words you left out.
- Read one line at a time and keep the rest of the paper covered.
- Check for neatness.
- If you write your work by hand, make sure others can read it.
- Check for sentence fragments by reading each sentence one word at a time.
- Use the grammar section of this handbook to look up things you are not sure of.
- Use proofreader's marks to show changes.

Proofreader's Marks

≡	Capitalize.
⊙	Add a period.
∧	Add something.
⋏	Add a comma.
⩔⩔	Add quotation marks.
ℓ	Take out something.
⋏	Replace something.
tr ∿	Trade places.
◯	Spell correctly.
⁋	Indent paragraph.
/	Make a lowercase letter.

PROOFREADING STRATEGIES

USING COMPUTERS

When you polish your writing, using a computer can help you

- **move words and sentences easily.**
- **check your spelling.**
- **find a more exact word.**

Thesaurus

Some word processing programs have a **thesaurus** that suggests vivid words you can use to replace overused words.

Spell-Check

A **spell-check** program will find misspelled words. However, a computer will miss words that are spelled correctly but used incorrectly. Here are some examples.

Tricky came out <u>two</u> get the treat.
Two is a real word used incorrectly here.

The dog ran under a <u>brush</u>.
Bush is the correct word, but *brush* is spelled correctly as a word.

Computers help, but they can't do it all.

A REVISED AND PROOFREAD DRAFT

Look at the changes one writer made to this first draft. The revisions are shown in blue ink. The proofreading changes are shown in red.

Lee ran out the door. It was his sister Tina. He had heard a scream. The garden was a disaster area. And Tricky was the cause.

Tricky was wet. Tricky was muddy. Lee made a grab for Tricky who was slipery, but the dog's muddy fur made her hard to hold. The dog ran under a brush. Tina had a idea. she got a bone. She held it in front of Trickys nose. When tricky came out two get the treat, Tina was ready. Lee was ready. They caught it!

Edits shown in the draft (handwritten):
- nervously into the yard. He was worried and scared.
- his sister Tina (circled)
- heard **a** scream (→ a, scream)
- disaster area**,** And
- his dog, Tricky
- Trickky → Tricky; Wet **and** Tricky
- grabbed her, but she
- **as** slipery → as; **p**; as an eel.
- squirmed (The dog ran → squirmed)
- rosebush (brush → rosebush)
- ¶ Then Tina had a**n** idea.
- soup (bone → soup); and dangled
- held it in front of Tricky's nose.
- tried (came out → tried) two → to
- **and** was ready. Lee was
- caught **her** it!

How do vivid verbs make this paragraph better?

How does the writer get rid of unnecessary words?

THE FINAL DRAFT

A final draft should be read one last time for errors.

Lee ran nervously into the yard. He was worried and scared. He had heard his sister Tina scream. The garden was a disaster area, and Tricky, his dog, was the cause.

Tricky was wet and muddy. Lee grabbed her, but she was as slippery as an eel. The dog squirmed under a rosebush.

Then Tina had an idea. She got a soup bone and dangled it in front of Tricky's nose. When Tricky tried to get the treat, Tina and Lee caught her!

The events are in clear order.

There is space at the top and at the side. Why is it a good idea to leave this space?

Publishing Your Writing

When authors publish their writing, they share it with others in some way. How you share your writing will depend on your task, your audience, and your purpose. Here are some ways to publish what you have written.

Publishing means sharing your work with others.

- Read your final draft aloud to a friend, a teacher, or your classmates.

- Turn a story into a play. Then work with others to perform it.

- Gather stories and poems written by classmates. Make a table of contents and create a class book.

- Make a cover and a title page for your own writing to turn it into a book.

- Illustrate a story to make it into a picture book.

- Give an oral report.

- Send a disk with your writing on it to a friend who can read it at a computer terminal.

Here are a few other ways to share your writing with others.

- Read your writing in front of a video camera.
- Make a tape recording of your work.
- Mail or fax your writing to the person you want to read it.
- Send your work to a publisher.
- Gather news stories, write headlines, and make a class newspaper.
- Add sound effects and background music to give a dramatic reading.
- Ask interested classmates to dance to or act out a story or poem as you read it.

What other ways can you think of to share your writing?

Use your imagination to find other ways to share your writing.

Writing Approaches

You write every day in different ways. You write for school assignments. You write when you jot down messages or make a list of things to do. You write alone and in a group. There are many different ways to write, but all help you sort ideas and think through problems.

WRITING IN A GROUP

One good way to discover ideas or answers to problems is to write as part of a group. Here are some suggested roles.

- The **Reader** reads aloud questions, directions, and other information.

- The **Questioner** ask questions.

- The **Recorder** takes notes, records answers, and writes the final draft.

- The **Checker** proofreads what the **Recorder** has written.

Writing in a group means teamwork.

SHARED WRITING

In shared writing, another person such as a teacher or a family member helps you think through your writing. He or she asks questions and records what you say. You choose the topic and the words you use.

WRITING TO LEARN

Writing to learn is a way of thinking on paper. You do not have to plan or edit this kind of writing. You do not need to publish it. You are writing to learn whenever you

- **make notes to compare two things.**
- **write a summary.**
- **write an observation.**
- **sort ideas into groups.**
- **make a judgment.**
- **tell what something means to you.**

Writing is a tool for thinking.

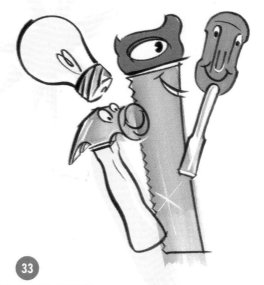

Writing to Learn Every Day

You can use writing to learn in these ways.

- **At the end of a discussion, jot down your thoughts. Think about what was said.**

- **As you begin an assignment, list questions you want answered.**

- **Write out a plan before you start a project.**

Learning Log

You can use writing as a tool for thinking when you take notes in a learning log. In the left column, write notes from your reading. In the right column, write thoughts and questions about your notes.

> *Write the questions you want answered.*

The Oregon Trail

Settlers traveled 2,000 miles northwest.	What kind of land did the people travel over?
Travelers packed all their belongings in one wagon.	What would I take? What would I leave behind?

Writing Forms

Writing to Entertain or Express

Performers may act, sing, or dance to entertain an audience and to express themselves. A writer has a similar purpose when writing to **entertain** readers or to **express** feelings. If you like to tell stories, read poetry, or act, you can put your ideas on paper.

PREWRITING

Choosing a Topic

- Will my characters be real or imaginary?

- What might make a good story, folktale, poem, or play?

Gathering and Organizing Details

- What is my setting?

- Who are my characters?

- What problem will the characters have?

- Will using a graphic organizer help me?

A story map or a time line can help you put events in order.

DRAFTING

- Am I using my prewriting notes?
- Does my story have a beginning, a middle, and an ending?
- Do my characters solve their problem?

RESPONDING AND REVISING

- Have I used vivid words?
- Are my events in order?

PROOFREADING

- Have I made errors in grammar or spelling?
- Have I checked for other mistakes?

PUBLISHING

- Is my final copy neatly written or typed?
- What is the best way to share my work?

EXPRESSIVE WRITING MODELS

MODEL: STORY

*In a **story**, a writer tells about one main idea. A story has characters, a plot, and a setting. It also has a beginning, a middle, and an ending.*

title

**beginning
(with characters,
setting, problem)**

middle

Little Mouse Bells the Cat

The attic mice were all good friends, but they lived in fear of Claws, the house cat. Many mice had damaged tails because of Claws.

"If only we could hear him coming, we'd have time to run away," said Little Mouse.

"We once had a plan to put a bell around his neck," said Bent-Tail.

"That's a great idea," cried Little Mouse. "Why didn't you do it?"

"I bent my tail trying," said Bent-Tail.

Just then, Knotted-Tail ran in. "That cat took my cheese!" he cried.

Suddenly, Little Mouse had an idea. She ran to her nest, where she had hidden a bell. She slipped it onto a piece of ribbon. Then she put it on and went downstairs.

Claws heard her coming. "What's making that lovely noise?" he asked.

"It's my wonderful new necklace," squeaked Little Mouse.

"I want it," hissed the cat. "Give it to me, now!"

"Take it!" yelled Little Mouse, as she yanked off the necklace and ran away.

ending (with problem solved)

Claws put on his new necklace. He purred when he heard the lovely noise. From that day on, the mice could hear Claws coming.

NARRATIVE WRITING

MODEL: DIALOGUE

*In a **dialogue**, a writer tells the exact words that one person or character says to another. Put the exact words between quotation marks (" "). Separate the quotation from the rest of the sentence with a comma or an end mark.*

exact words

new paragraph started with new speaker

"What's making that lovely noise?" Claws asked.

"It's my wonderful new necklace," squeaked Little Mouse in fear.

"I want it," hissed the cat. "Give it to me, now!"

"Take it!" yelled Little Mouse, as she yanked off the necklace and ran away.

40

NARRATIVE WRITING

*A **poem** paints a picture or expresses a feeling with words. It may repeat word or letter sounds and have **rhyme**. A poem often has a definite **rhythm**, or beat.*

Rhymed Poem

Cat and Mouse

The mouse poked out her tiny <u>head</u>.
"Look and listen," her mother <u>said</u>.
She heard a bell, and that was <u>that</u>.
The clever mouse escaped the <u>cat</u>.

title

words that rhyme
(underlined)

Unrhymed Poem

Not all poems rhyme. Read how the poem might be written without rhyme.

Cat and Mouse

<u>Like</u> a guard watching for danger,
the mouse peeked around for the cat.

<u>Like</u> an alarm ringing out a warning, the cat's bell signaled the mouse.

<u>As</u> quick <u>as</u> an eye blink, the mouse disappeared.

title

word that compares
(underlined)

MODEL: PLAY

*A **play** is a story you can act out. It has characters, a setting, and a plot. In a play, the conversation is called **dialogue.** The **stage directions** tell the characters how to move, act, and speak.*

title

Little Mouse Bells the Cat

NARRATOR: The attic mice fear Claws, the nasty and very quiet house cat. Claws sneaks up on the mice and takes their food. Many mice have damaged tails because of Claws. One even has a bent tail! What will the mice do?

dialogue

LITTLE MOUSE (sadly): If we could hear him coming, we'd have time to run away.

BENT-TAIL (thoughtfully): We once had a plan to make it easy to hear him coming. I remember! We wanted to put a bell around his nasty neck.

LITTLE MOUSE (excitedly): That's a great idea. Why didn't you do it?

BENT-TAIL (sadly): I bent my tail trying.

LITTLE MOUSE (bravely): Well, I'll find a way to bell that cat.

KNOTTED-TAIL (running in): That cat just took my lunch! He wants everything we have!

LITTLE MOUSE (excitedly): You just gave me an idea.

KNOTTED-TAIL (curiously): What is it?

LITTLE MOUSE (explaining): I'll take a bell I found and put it on this ribbon. (makes a necklace) You said Claws wants everything we have. Watch this!

stage directions

NARRATOR: Little Mouse puts on the necklace and goes out. Claws hears the mouse coming.

CLAWS: Who's making that music?

LITTLE MOUSE (boasting): It's my necklace.

CLAWS: (hissing): Give it to me, now!

LITTLE MOUSE (throwing the necklace and running away): Take it!

CLAWS (speaking to himself): I love the music my new necklace makes.

ALL THE MICE (whispering to the audience): We love it, too!

Writing to Describe

Have you ever written about a pet you own, a place you visited, or a meal you liked? If you have, your purpose for writing was to **describe.** In a description, you use details to help your audience see, feel, hear, and maybe even taste and smell what you are describing. Think about these questions when you are writing to describe.

Important! Include details that tell about the senses.

PREWRITING

Choosing a Topic

- **Will I write about a person, a place, or a thing?**

- **Do I know the topic well?**

- **Will my audience find this topic interesting?**

Gathering and Organizing Details

- **What details will I use?**

- **Will my details appeal to the senses?**

MODEL: DESCRIPTIVE PARAGRAPH

*A **descriptive paragraph** paints a word picture. It describes a person, a place, an object, or an event.*

topic sentence

Last fall, the air was <u>crisp</u> and <u>cool</u> as Sam and his big brother waited for the parade to pass. Suddenly, they heard the <u>thump</u> of the <u>big</u> school drum. The parade was coming! Jerry is <u>tall</u>, but even he had trouble seeing over all the people. Beside Jerry a <u>little</u> girl with a <u>sweet—smelling jelly</u> doughnut was crying. She couldn't see a thing. Jerry put her on his shoulders. Then she could see all the <u>high—stepping</u> marchers. The little girl <u>squealed</u> with delight!

detail sentences

words that appeal to the senses (underlined)

DRAFTING

- What will my topic sentence be?
- Do all my details describe the topic?

RESPONDING AND REVISING

- Does my topic sentence tell whom or what I am describing?
- Do my details appeal to the senses?
- What other details can I add?

PROOFREADING

- Have I spelled every word correctly?
- Have I used capitalization and punctuation correctly?

PUBLISHING

- How can I share my writing with others?
- Will a picture make my description clearer?

DESCRIPTIVE WRITING MODELS

Descriptive Paragraph, page 46

Character Sketch, page 47

MODEL: CHARACTER SKETCH

*In a **character sketch,** a writer describes a real or an imaginary person.*

topic sentence

    In the book <u>The Best Fall</u>, Jerry Adams is a tall but shy student at Midvale School and Sam's big brother. It isn't easy for Jerry to decide between the school band and the football team. Jerry chooses the school band, but he really wants

how character acts

to be a part of football, too. Jerry solves his problem in a clever way.

special qualities

Every Saturday, he helps coach Sam and the other third-graders on the little league football team. Jerry is one of the kindest and smartest characters in the whole book.

iting to Inform

What would you like to know more about? What information would you like to share with others? When you share this information in writing, you are writing to **inform**. Think about these questions when you are writing to inform.

PREWRITING

Choosing a Topic

- **Will I write about something I know or something new?**

- **What facts do I need to include?**

Gathering Information

- **Where can I find information on this topic?**

- **What sources can I use?**

DRAFTING

- **Am I including background knowledge my audience needs?**

- **Does my topic sentence state the main idea?**

RESPONDING AND REVISING

- Have I presented information clearly and in the right order?
- What details can I add or leave out?

PROOFREADING

- Have I spelled proper nouns and technical words correctly?
- Did I capitalize all proper nouns?

PUBLISHING

- How will I share my work with others?
- What visual materials will help?

MODEL: PERSONAL NARRATIVE

*In a **personal narrative**, a writer tells about an experience in his or her life.*

strong beginning

Why was I named Cameroon Pelée? I never thought about it until a friend asked how I had gotten my name. I didn't know, so I went home to search for answers. First, I sat down to think. Then my sister Helen came in. She was born on the day a volcano named Mount Saint Helens erupted. That's how she got her name. I asked her how I had gotten mine. She said that I got my name the same way she did. It's true. I looked it up. I was born on the same day a volcano erupted in Cameroon, Africa.

middle that describes events in time order

ending

*A **paragraph of information** gives facts about one topic. It has a topic sentence that tells the main idea. At least two detail sentences give facts about the main idea.*

title

topic sentence

facts

The Peak of Perfection

Mount Cameroon is a special mountain in Africa. It is the highest mountain in western Africa and an active volcano. The last time Mount Cameroon erupted was over 30 years ago. Ash that came out of the volcano turned into rich soil. Farmers now grow tea, rubber trees, and cocoa in that soil. Mount Cameroon is also special because it is one of the wettest places on earth. More than 400 inches of rain fall there each year.

MODEL: HOW-TO PARAGRAPH

*A **how-to paragraph** gives directions or explains how to do something. Steps are given in time order.*

How to Make a Volcano

topic sentence

time-order words (underlined here) in steps

You can make a small volcano at home with an adult's help. You will need a pan, a plastic bottle, red food coloring, a bottle of vinegar, baking soda, and some sand. <u>First</u>, add a few drops of food coloring to the vinegar. <u>Next</u>, fill the plastic bottle halfway with baking soda and place it in the middle of the pan. Pile the sand around the bottle. <u>Finally</u>, have your adult family member quickly pour the vinegar into the hole. Stand back, and let the volcano erupt.

MODEL: PARAGRAPH THAT COMPARES

*In a **paragraph that compares,** a writer shows how people, places, or things are alike.*

topic sentence

detail sentences with clear examples of things that are alike

My sister Helen and I are alike in many ways. Both of us have curly black hair and brown eyes. We also share a sense of humor and enjoy telling jokes and stories to our friends. What makes us most alike is the way we got our names. Both Helen and I were named after volcanoes that erupted on the day we were born!

MODEL: PARAGRAPH THAT CONTRASTS

In a **paragraph that contrasts,** *a writer shows how people, places, or things are different.*

topic sentence

detail sentences with clear examples of differences

My sister Helen and I are different in a couple of ways. First, she is already in high school. Her school experience is helpful when she helps me figure out a tough class assignment. Another difference is that I always know where all our things are, but she always loses things. I don't know how Helen could find anything at all without me.

EXPOSITORY WRITING

MODEL: WRITING FOR MATH

When you write a word problem or express a math equation in words, you are **writing for math.** Any time you write a word problem, always include enough information to solve it.

Before it erupted on May 18, 1980, Mount Saint Helens was 9,677 feet high. After it erupted, it was 8,364 feet high. How much height did Mount Saint Helens lose?

Use the Problem-Solving Think Along™ below to help you use writing to solve problems.

Understand

1. Retell the problem in your own words.
2. Reword the question as a fill-in-the-blank sentence.
3. List the information given.

Plan

4. List problem-solving strategies you can use.
5. Predict what your answer will be.

Solve

6. Show how you solved the problem.
7. Write your answer in a complete sentence.

Look Back

8. Tell how you know your answer is reasonable.
9. Describe another way you could have solved the problem.

MODEL: WRITING FOR SCIENCE

*When you write what you observe during an experiment, you are **writing for science**. Include a title, a purpose, materials, the procedure, observations, and conclusions.*

A Homemade Volcano

Purpose: To make a model volcano.

Materials: large pan, bottle, safety goggles, red food coloring, vinegar, baking soda, sand.

Procedure
1. Put on safety goggles.
2. Add red food coloring to the vinegar and set it aside.
3. Half-fill the bottle with baking soda.
4. Place the bottle in the pan.
5. Pile sand around the bottle.
6. Have an adult put on safety goggles and quickly pour the vinegar into the bottle. Observe the eruption.

Observations
   When the vinegar touched the baking soda, red foam bubbled up out of the bottle and down the volcano's sides.

Conclusion
   Volcanoes erupt from deep inside.

*In a **news story,** a reporter gives information to an audience. A news story tells who, what, when, where, why, and sometimes how.*

*Often a reporter conducts an **interview** to check story facts or learn more facts. A reporter takes notes and avoids questions with only "yes" or "no" answers.*

headline

Local Scientist Discusses Volcanoes

Who?
What?

Dr. Vesuvius Pelée will give a talk about his recent experiments near Mount Pinatubo in the Philippines. The talk will be given at the

Where?
When?

Hampton Public Library on Monday, November 21, at 1:30 p.m.

Why?

Dr. Pelée's interest in this field began when he learned as a child that both his names were also names of volcanoes.

RESEARCH REPORT

*To write a **research report**, a writer gathers facts from several sources, takes notes, and makes an **outline**. The notes and outline are used to write the report. The writer lists the sources at the end of the report.*

Outline

An outline follows a certain form. Roman numerals show the main ideas. Letters show the subtopics.

**Scientists Predict
Volcanic Eruptions**

I. Information studied
    A. Volcano's history
    B. Rising ground
    C. Gases in the air
II. Kinds of warnings
    A. Before eruption
    B. Volcano drills

*A **research report** gives facts about a topic. This short report follows the outline on page 58. Reports can be several pages long.*

title

Scientists Predict Volcanic Eruptions

main topic

facts about subtopics

Scientists are getting better at telling when a volcano will erupt. One way they can tell is to study how often it has erupted before. Another way they can tell is to use a special instrument called a <u>tiltmeter</u>. They use this instrument to measure whether the ground is rising. Scientists also use an instrument called a <u>gas detector</u>. It measures the amount of gas in the air.

main topic

facts about subtopics

When scientists think an eruption is coming, they warn people and tell them to leave. In parts of Japan and Ecuador, towns conduct volcano drills. These are like fire drills. Scientists have saved many lives with their research.

Writing to Persuade

Have you ever tried to change someone's mind? If you have, your purpose was to **persuade** the other person to think like you. When you write to persuade, you want your audience to agree with you and even take action. Here are some things to think about when your purpose for writing is to persuade.

Save your best facts for last when you write to persuade.

PREWRITING

Choosing a Topic

- **What do I feel strongly about?**
- **Will my audience find this topic interesting?**

Gathering and Organizing Details

- **What facts will I use to support my opinion?**
- **Which is the most important fact?**

DRAFTING

- Do I have a topic sentence?
- Is my opinion clear?
- Did I put my strongest fact last?

RESPONDING AND REVISING

- Do I need to state my opinions or facts more clearly?
- Have I convinced my audience?

PROOFREADING

- Have I checked for spelling mistakes?
- Have I used correct grammar and punctuation?

PUBLISHING

- What's the best way to present my work?
- Will photographs, charts, or graphs help me make a stronger statement?

MODEL: PERSUASIVE PARAGRAPH

*In a **persuasive paragraph,** a writer tries to make readers agree with his or her opinion.*

opinion in topic sentence

reasons and facts

strongest reason last

restated opinion or call for action

    Whale–watching is good for people and for the environment. Many people have begun working for earth–friendly causes after sailing near whales. Also, these intelligent animals seem to like the visitors. Tourists describe excitedly how whales come up to the boats to be touched. Most important, whale–watching helps people learn how valuable and beautiful these mysterious mammals are. Everyone is helped by a whale–watching trip. Find out more about one today!

*A **book review** tells briefly what a book is about without telling the ending. It also gives the writer's opinion of the book. Finally, it says whether others should read it.*

title

author

main character

setting

main idea of book

whether others should read it

Humphrey the Lost Whale

The book Humphrey the Lost Whale by Wendy Tokuda and Richard Hall tells the true story of a young whale that took a wrong turn. In the book, people were at first surprised and pleased to see a whale in San Francisco Bay. Then Humphrey headed up the Sacramento River. People soon realized he was lost. Hundreds of people worked together to get Humphrey back to the ocean. This story will make you cheer. Read this book, and share it with a friend.

MODEL: TELEVISION OR MOVIE REVIEW

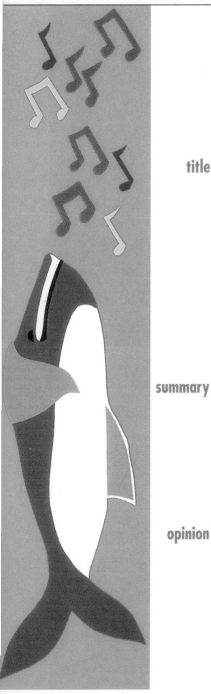

*A **television review** or a **movie review** tells what a program or a movie is about. The review also gives the writer's opinion of the program or movie and tells whether others should view it.*

title

<u>The Song of the Whale</u>

<u>The Song of the Whale</u> is a television program about humpback whales, their habitat, and how they live. The wonderful camera work takes viewers into the underwater world of humpback whales. There

summary

are scenes of the whales swimming, feeding, and raising their young. Viewers hear their songs and learn what they mean. You can tune in to your local public television station this

opinion

Tuesday at 7:30 P.M. to see this fine program. You won't want to miss it!

*In a **speech** or an **oral report**, a s
information with an audience. The
also try to persuade the audience t*

*A speaker often uses an outline an
give the report. A speaker sometim
slides, or pictures as well.*

You

lette

than

invit

**notes
for topic**

> I. Baleen whales
> a. Have no teet
> B. Sift krill t
>   filter

wri

wri

hel

Ch

• V

• V
 a

**notes expanded into
oral report
(actual words)**

"Many people believe it is in
the whales, but not many peopl
these mysterious mammals. For
you know that some kinds of wh
teeth? Baleen whales don't need
tiny krill that are their main food
through a filter called baleen.

...ou don't write only for school assignments.
...robably write these kinds of things, too:

...s	journal entries	notes
...-you notes	lists	summaries
...tions	messages	

...ou don't often need all the steps of the
...ng process for these kinds of everyday
...ng. Sometimes, though, you might find it
...ul to ask yourself questions such as these.

Most everyday writing is informal. Write freely!

Things to do:

P R E W R I T I N G

...sing a Topic

...o is my audience?

...at are my task
...d my purpose?

Gathering and Organizing Details

- **What information do I need to include?**

- **Do I need to list dates, times, addresses, or telephone numbers?**

...are
...nvited

Thank you

Grocery list:
1. apples
2. milk
3. eggs
4. carrots
5. juice
6. tomatoes

DRAFTING

- Have I included all the needed parts?
- Are events in the right order?

RESPONDING AND REVISING

- Did I accomplish my task and my purpose?
- Are there details I want to add or cut?

PROOFREADING

- Are names and addresses spelled correctly?
- Do I need to worry about grammar or punctuation?

PUBLISHING

- Do I need to publish this, or is it just for me?
- Will I write my final copy by hand?
- Do I need an envelope?
- Have I included all the needed parts?

EVERYDAY WRITING MODELS

MODEL: JOURNAL

*A **journal** is a place where a writer records events, ideas, and feelings. Each dated piece in the journal is called an **entry**.*

date

what happened

why it is important

March 5, 1995

Today when I came home from school, I had a surprise. Grandma was there! She decided to visit for my 7-year, 11-month birthday because she won't be able to come for my real birthday. On my real birthday, she'll be in California helping my Aunt Jenny take care of a new baby. Grandma also gave me an early birthday present. Now I have the hamster I've always wanted. I named him Sandy.

A **dialogue journal** is a journal in which you exchange ideas and feelings with someone else. You might share a dialogue journal with a teacher, a friend, or a family member.

date

March 6, 1995

student's journal comment

Yesterday my grandmother gave me an early birthday present. She brought me a hamster. As much as I love him, I was surprised when he ran around in his squeaky exercise wheel all night.

signature

Mimi

date

March 8, 1995

teacher's response

It sounds like you have a healthy, normal hamster. Hamsters sleep during the day and eat, work, and play at night. What's his name?

signature

Ms. Rhodes

MODEL: FRIENDLY LETTER

A person writes to someone he or she knows in a **friendly letter.** *A friendly letter has five parts: a* heading, *a* greeting, *a* body, *a* closing, *and a* signature. *In the heading, the writer includes a comma between the name of the city and state and between the day of the month and the year.*

heading

27 Green Street
Burlington, NC 27215
April 10, 1995

greeting

Dear Grandma,

body

Sandy and I are fine. Last night he was a busy hamster rearranging the wood shavings in his habitat. I love watching him. Please give Aunt Jenny a hug and a kiss for me.

closing
signature

Love,
Mimi

*In an **invitation,** a writer asks someone to a party or another event. A letter of invitation has the same parts as a friendly letter. It also tells what the event is, when it will be, and where it will take place. Also, it asks for a response.*

heading

27 Green Street
Burlington, NC 27215
April 10, 1995

greeting

Dear Wanda,

body

Please come to a sleepover party this weekend at my house. My mom will pick you up on Friday. On Saturday we will go skating. I hope you can come. Please call by Wednesday to let me know.

closing
signature

Your friend,
Mimi

MODEL: THANK-YOU NOTE

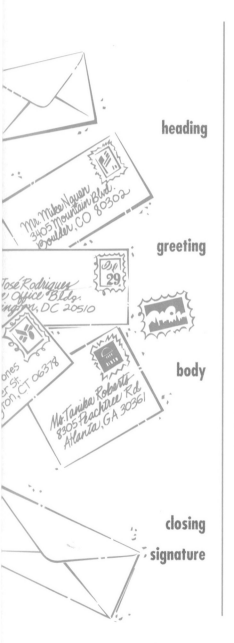

*When someone helps you in some way, it is good manners to write a **thank-you note**.*

heading

27 Green Street
Burlington, NC 27215
April 15, 1995

greeting

Dear Sheila,

body

Thank you for helping me catch my hamster Sandy this weekend. I was afraid I had lost him forever. Your idea to put out some food and water at night was a good one.
I hope you can visit again soon. I promise to leave Sandy in his habitat next time.

closing

Your friend,

signature

Mimi

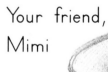

DESCRIPTIVE/NARRATIVE WRITING

*A letter or a note is sent in an **envelope.** The envelope shows the* receiver's address *and the* return address. *The address needs a* postal abbreviation *for the state and a* ZIP code.

return address

receiver's address

Mimi Pappas
27 Green Street
Burlington, NC 27215

Sheila Wilson
601 East Broadway
Burlington, NC 27215

Postal Abbreviations

Alabama AL	Kentucky KY	Ohio OH
Alaska AK	Louisiana LA	Oklahoma OK
Arizona AZ	Maine ME	Oregon OR
Arkansas AR	Maryland MD	Pennsylvania PA
California CA	Massachusetts MA	Rhode Island RI
Colorado CO	Michigan MI	South Carolina SC
Connecticut CT	Minnesota MN	South Dakota SD
Delaware DE	Mississippi MS	Tennessee TN
District of	Missouri MO	Texas TX
Columbia DC	Montana MT	Utah UT
Florida FL	Nebraska NE	Vermont VT
Georgia GA	Nevada NV	Virginia VA
Hawaii HI	New Hampshire NH	Washington WA
Idaho ID	New Jersey NJ	West Virginia WV
Illinois IL	New Mexico NM	Wisconsin WI
Indiana IN	New York NY	Wyoming WY
Iowa IA	North Carolina NC	
Kansas KS	North Dakota ND	

M O D E L :   M E S S A G E

*A **message** states information that is given in person or by telephone. It tells who the message is for and what it is about. Ask the caller to spell or repeat any part that is not clear.*

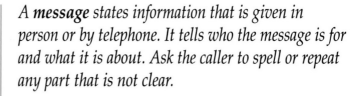

day and time

Tuesday
11:30 a.m.

receiver's name

message

Mimi,

    Mr. Sanchez from the pet store called. The tunnel tube brush is in.

name and telephone number of caller

You can call him at 555-1234 until 6 P.M. Someone else wants it if you don't.

your name

            Gus

*You fill in information on a **form** when you enter a contest, order from a catalog, or join a club. When you fill out a form, you should do these things.*

- **Read the directions before you begin.**

- **Write neatly and clearly.**

- **Give all the information the form asks for.**

- **Write everything in the correct space.**

Valley Pet Shop Order Form

Please print using a pen.

Name ___ Pappas ___ Mimi
            Last   First

Address ___ 27 Green Street ___ 27215
             Number & Street   Zip Code

             NC
             State

Burlington   555-2445
City

Telephone

Item	Description	Total Number
VPS18	tunnel tube brush	1
VPS12	hamster food bags	2

MODEL: NOTES

Notes are a kind of writing that helps you remember things. You take notes in class to help you remember what you hear or read. You also take notes to do research for a report or to study for a test.

One good way to take notes is to write on index cards. Use one card for each main idea. Add facts below the main idea. Use your own words. Write the source of the information on the card.

topic

main idea as question

facts

source

HAMSTERS

What are some facts about hamsters?

rodents	short tail
active at night	desert animals
have cheek pouches	like to burrow
thick fur	

<u>Your Pet Hamster</u> by Tim Barnes, p. 27

*A **summary** helps the writer remember main points. A summary can be about information from a book, an article, a film, a talk, or what you observe. It is written in the writer's own words. It has a main idea and a few important details.*

sample source

Hamster is the common name for any of 14 species of rodents. These animals have cheek pouches that they use to hold and carry large amounts of food such as seeds. They also have thick fur and short tails. Hamsters are nocturnal, or active at night. They are desert animals and dig burrows with several compartments. The golden hamster from Syria and the dwarf hamster from Asia make excellent house pets that are easy to care for.

summary

Hamsters are rodents. They have thick fur, short tails, and cheek pouches to hold and carry food. They are active at night but make great house pets.

77

Writing for a Test

Some kinds of test questions ask for a written response. They check whether you can express ideas, organize thoughts, write for a specific task and purpose, and use correct grammar. Remember these things when writing for a test.

BEFORE THE TEST

- Listen carefully to *all* the directions your teacher or test-giver gives you.

- Read all written directions carefully.

- Ask any questions you have. (You might not be allowed to talk once the test starts.)

- Have several pens or sharpened pencils on hand.

- If you are allowed, read each item on the test before you begin.

DURING THE TEST

- Take time to identify your task, audience, and purpose.

- Organize your thoughts before you write.

- Write neatly and clearly.

- If you need help, raise your hand. Don't call out or get up.

AFTER THE TEST

- If you finish before time is up, go back and make final corrections.

- Follow directions given at the beginning for what to do at the end of the test. You may have to sit quietly while others finish.

TIMED WRITING

You have probably taken timed tests before. But what are some ways to do well during a timed writing test? Follow these tips to make a timed test go more smoothly:

- **Stay calm. Take a deep breath and relax.**

- **For a writing test, remember to check your task and your purpose. (Unless you are told otherwise, your audience is the person who will read the test.)**

- **Plan how you will use your time. If this is a writing test, decide how much time you need to spend prewriting, drafting, revising, proofreading, and writing the final draft.**

- **If you begin to run out of time, decide if you can combine some steps. Your goal is to finish.**

WRITTEN PROMPT

A **written prompt** is a statement or a question that asks you to complete a writing task. The prompt on this page asks you to write a personal narrative.

Almost everyone has been to or has imagined a favorite place.

Think about your own experience in a favorite place. You may have been with many people, with a special friend, or by yourself. You may have been in a room or outdoors.

Now tell a story to your reader about what happened to you in this favorite place.

NARRATIVE WRITING

These prompts ask the writer to "tell a story."

PERSUASIVE WRITING

These prompts ask the writer to "convince or persuade."

EXPOSITORY WRITING

These prompts ask the writer to "tell or explain why."

DESCRIPTIVE WRITING

These prompts ask the writer to "describe."

PICTURE PROMPT

A **picture prompt** is a statement or a question about a picture. It asks the writer to tell something about the picture. The prompt tells the purpose for writing. Here is an example of a picture prompt that asks the writer to use description:

Picture yourself in this scene. Write a composition for your teacher in which you describe what you see.

Grammar, Usage, and Mechanics

GRAMMAR

USAGE

MECHANICS

SENTENCES

A *sentence* is a group of words that tells a complete thought. The words in a sentence should be in an order that makes sense. Begin every sentence with a capital letter, and end it with an end mark.

Most plants grow from seeds.

A fruit tree's seeds are usually found inside the fruit.

The seeds of an apple tree are in the apple's core.

A strawberry's seeds are on its skin.

The strawberry is an unusual fruit.

Exercise 1

Read each group of words. Tell whether each group is a sentence.

1. Some seeds grow best in warm places.
2. The banana is one tropical fruit.
3. A banana's seeds look like tiny black specks.
4. Taste sweet and fresh.
5. Many people order seeds from catalogs.
6. People on farms.
7. A vegetable garden is fun to grow.
8. Beans grow quickly.
9. Anyone can spot a giant squash.
10. Tomatoes, cabbage, and corn.

For additional practice, turn to pages 170–171.

Writing Application

Think of three kinds of seeds. Write a sentence telling about each kind.

SENTENCES

STATEMENT

A *statement* is a sentence that tells something.
Use a period (.) at the end of a statement.

Luther Burbank was a famous gardener.

He spent his life studying plants.

Burbank developed a special blackberry.

Blackberries are a popular fruit.

QUESTION

A *question* is a sentence that asks something.
Use a question mark (?) at the end of a question.

Where did Luther Burbank live?

Can I visit the Luther Burbank Gardens?

What else did Luther Burbank do?

How did the Burbank potato get its name?

Exercise 2

Read each sentence. Tell whether it is a statement or a question.

1. Luther Burbank developed a fruit called the plumcot.
2. How did he develop such a fruit?
3. He put the pollen from one plant onto another plant.
4. The plumcot is part Japanese plum and part apricot.
5. What do you think a plumcot looks like?
6. A plumcot can be yellow, pink, red, or white.
7. Do you know what a plum tastes like?
8. Luther Burbank developed a plum that tastes like a pear.
9. How many plants did Luther Burbank grow?
10. He grew thousands of plants for each experiment.

For additional practice, turn to pages 172–173.

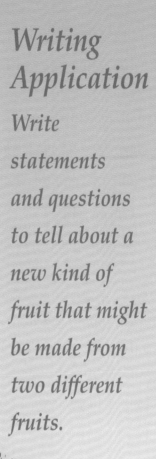

Writing Application

Write statements and questions to tell about a new kind of fruit that might be made from two different fruits.

SENTENCES

EXCLAMATION

An *exclamation* is a sentence that shows strong feeling. Use an exclamation point (!) at the end of an exclamation.

Wow, what a huge blackberry!

What big thorns this bush has!

I stuck myself!

What a delicious berry this is!

COMMAND

A *command* is a sentence that gives an order or a direction. Use a period (.) at the end of a command.

Look at these berries.

Don't pick those.

Forget about the sour berries.

Let the seeds grow into new plants.

Exercise 3

Read each sentence. Tell whether it is an exclamation or a command.

1. Your garden is so beautiful!
2. What a lot of work it is, too!
3. Please grow pumpkins.
4. Plant peppers, too.
5. Order the seeds from this catalog.
6. Put the weeds in that bag.
7. You're making me nervous!
8. Please don't order me around.
9. What lovely cabbages those are!
10. Wow, what a great visit this has been!

For additional practice, turn to pages 174–175.

Writing Application

Use four kinds of sentences to write about some vegetables you would like to grow.

SENTENCE PARTS

SUBJECT

Every sentence has a *subject.* The subject is the part of the sentence that tells the person or thing the sentence is about. The subject is usually at the beginning of a sentence.

Seeds travel in different ways.

Birds eat fruit from trees and vines.

They drop the seeds onto the ground.

Some of these seeds grow into plants.

Exercise 4

Tell what the subject is in each sentence.

1. Some seeds are carried by the wind.
2. Dandelion seeds are light and puffy.
3. The wind carries them a long way.
4. They float through the air.
5. Pioneers carried seeds with them.
6. These settlers planted the seeds.
7. Some families planned orchards.
8. The wilderness disappeared slowly.
9. Many plants make hundreds of seeds.
10. Small seedlings grow quickly into trees.

For additional practice, turn to pages 176–177.

PREDICATE

Every sentence has a *predicate.* The predicate is the part of the sentence that tells what the subject of the sentence is or does. The predicate is usually the last part of the sentence.

Sam Sanders *is the bravest kid in my class.*

Her first name *is short for Samantha.*

We *gave her this nickname.*

Sam *thinks of a new adventure every week.*

Exercise 5

Tell what the predicate is in each sentence.

1. Sam climbed Mount Whitney.
2. Mount Whitney is in California.
3. Sam went there with her father.
4. They climbed for one whole day.
5. Sam took pictures of snow at the top.
6. Sam went rafting on the Snake River.
7. The river bucked like a wild horse.
8. She loved the exciting ride.
9. Sam and her dad also explore caves.
10. Her next goal is surfing.

For additional practice, turn to pages 178–179.

For additional practice, turn to pages 178–179.

Writing Application

Write about an outdoor adventure you would like to take part in. Underline your predicates.

NOUNS

NOUN

A *noun* is a word that names a person, a place, or a thing.

leader	theater	piano
musician	downtown	rhythm
dancer	park	coat

Exercise 6

Find the noun or nouns in each sentence.

1. That guitar has a smooth sound.
2. Its owner likes the tune.
3. The orchestra is quiet now.
4. The new conductor steps onto the stage.
5. The woman introduces her guest.
6. A man plucks each string of his violin.
7. The audience listens to his fine music.
8. A singer sings a fast song.
9. One person taps her feet to its rhythm.
10. When each artist ends a song, the crowd claps.

For additional practice, turn to pages 180–181.

COMMON NOUN

A *common noun* names any person, place, or thing. A common noun begins with a lowercase letter.

A *composer* writes *music.*

My *father* enjoys the *beat* of a big *band.*

My best *friend* likes to listen in his *home.*

Exercise 7

Read each sentence. Find the common nouns.

1. Has your family ever been to a musical?
2. Each main actor acts and sings on a stage.
3. One popular story is about a boy who won't grow up.
4. This play is performed in many cities.
5. A movie was also made for television.
6. Who remembers the name of that film?
7. A girl plays the main role.
8. A great voice is a big help.
9. That lady really sings her part well.
10. The character flies through the air.

For additional practice, turn to pages 182–183.

For additional practice, turn to pages 182–183.

Writing Application

Use common nouns to write about your favorite music.

NOUNS

PROPER NOUN

A *proper noun* names a particular person, place, or thing. Begin each important word of a proper noun with a capital letter.

The telephone near *Susie* plays music when it rings.

Alexander Graham Bell invented the telephone.

In 1847 he was born in *Edinburgh, Scotland.*

Exercise 8

Read each sentence. Tell which words are proper nouns.

1. In 1872 Bell opened a school in Boston, Massachusetts.
2. A year later he taught at Boston University.
3. He developed the idea for the telephone in Brantford, Canada.
4. Thomas Edison proved that electricity carries sound.
5. Bell met a man named Thomas Watson in an electrical shop.
6. Their idea for a telephone began to work in March 1876.

For additional practice, turn to pages 184–185.

Hello! My name is Igor Sobolevskiy [ē´gôr sō•bō•lefs´kē], and I'm from Moscow, the capital city of Russia. In Russia, there is more than one right way to spell the name of a place. It all depends on how the name is used.

Let's take Moscow, for example. On a Russian map it is spelled MOCKBA. That's pronounced [mäsk•vä´]. Saying that someone lives in a place changes the way the name of that place is spelled. If I say, "Igor used to live in Moscow," the city name is spelled MOCKBE. You would pronounce it [mäsk•vye´].

NOUNS

A *singular noun* names one person, one place, or one thing.

student	classroom	apple
neighbor	house	ruler
friend	bus	performance
princess	porch	chorus

A *plural noun* names more than one person, place, or thing. Make most nouns plural by adding *s* or *es*.

students	classrooms	apples
neighbors	houses	rulers
friends	buses	performances
princesses	porches	choruses

Exercise 9

Read these sentences. Tell which nouns are singular and which are plural.

1. Most schools once had only one room.
2. A child might share the same space with older students.
3. Each classroom had a stove.
4. The teacher often chopped logs for it.
5. Many students walked for miles to school.
6. How did the girls and boys stay warm?
7. Sometimes they carried hot potatoes in their pockets.
8. A potato stays hot for a long time.
9. The youngsters kept their hands warm by holding these objects.
10. Then they ate these vegetables for their lunch!

For additional practice, turn to pages 186–187.

Writing Application

Use singular and plural nouns to write about things you see in your classroom.

NOUNS

To form the plural of a singular noun that ends with a consonant and *y*, change the *y* to *i* and add *es*.

Singular	Plural
city	cit*ies*
pony	pon*ies*
baby	bab*ies*
party	part*ies*
berry	berr*ies*
penny	penn*ies*

Writing
Application
*Use plural
nouns to write
about an
invention that
interests you.*

Exercise 10

Find the common nouns in these sentences.
Make each singular noun plural. Make each
plural noun singular.

1. Louis Braille was born near the city of Paris,
   France.
2. He was a healthy baby but later could not see.
3. Louis's family sent him away to be helped.
4. Louis wished that he could read stories.
5. After many tries, he developed a special code.
6. Today Braille is used in countries everywhere.

For additional practice, turn to pages 188–189.

NOUNS

Some nouns change their spelling in the plural form.

Singular	Plural
tooth	teeth
foot	feet
man	men
woman	women
child	children
mouse	mice
goose	geese
ox	oxen

Exercise 11

Tell the plural form of each underlined singular noun. Tell the singular form of each underlined plural noun.

1. My great-grandfather is the most interesting <u>man</u> I know.
2. He is almost ninety, but he is strong and quick on his <u>feet</u>.
3. He still has almost all his <u>teeth</u>.
4. Great-grandpa has eight <u>children</u>.
5. He has fourteen <u>grandchildren</u> and twenty-six <u>great-grandchildren</u>.
6. He spends time with every <u>child</u> in the family.
7. He told me all about the <u>geese</u> that fly over our house in the fall.
8. He taught my sister how to carve a <u>goose</u> out of soap.
9. Great-grandpa's marigolds are almost a <u>foot</u> tall!
10. When he is napping, I am as quiet as a <u>mouse</u>.

For additional practice, turn to pages 190–191.

For additional practice, turn to pages 190–191.

Writing Application

Use singular and plural nouns to write about a special man or woman.

NOUNS

POSSESSIVE NOUN

A *possessive noun* shows ownership. It tells what someone or something owns or has.

Angela's class visited a hospital.

They learned about a *doctor's* work.

They discovered that a *nurse's* job is very important.

"We care about all our *patients'* health," the doctor said.

"Every *person's* needs are important to us."

Exercise 12

Find the possessive noun in each sentence. Tell what belongs to that person or thing.

1. One girl's friend had an idea.
2. "The hospital's walls are bare," Roscoe said.
3. "That boy's room is filled with pictures," he continued.
4. "We'll draw pictures for the patients' rooms," Angela said.
5. "Maybe we can use the school's paintbrushes," Roger suggested.
6. The children met at Kimlee's house.
7. Her mother's studio was the perfect place for drawing.
8. "Look at Rosie's giant sunflower!" André said.
9. "The goldfish in Roscoe's painting are also pretty!" said Rosie.
10. "This is the class's best project yet!" Angela exclaimed.

For additional practice, turn to pages 192–193.

Writing Application

Use possessive nouns to write about an art project your class could do to help people feel better.

NOUNS

SINGULAR POSSESSIVE NOUN

A *singular possessive noun* shows ownership by one person or thing. Add an apostrophe (') and *s* to a singular noun to show ownership.

I tore off the big *box's* ribbon excitedly.

Aunt *Rose's* beautiful gift surprised me.

I loved the *quilt's* colorful patches.

Whenever I look at the quilt, I think of my *aunt's* crinkled smile.

Exercise 13

Find the singular possessive noun in each sentence.

1. Here is one of our family's Seminole traditions.
2. On each child's tenth birthday, he or she gets a quilted jacket.
3. Aunt Irene's sewing talent is great.
4. To make a jacket, she collects pieces of the child's old clothing.
5. Each jacket's colors are different.

For additional practice, turn to pages 194–195.

Hello. My name is Obaid Vicaruddin [ō•bād´ vē•kär´ōōd•dēn´], and I speak Urdu. The Urdu language is used in Pakistan and in some parts of India. People who speak Urdu can understand people who speak Hindi, the main language of India.

One way that Urdu is different from English is in the way you show possession. Here is an example. The Urdu word for dog is *coota*. If I am writing about my dog in English, I write *Obaid's dog* with an *'s* to show that it is mine.

If I am writing about my dog in Urdu, I write *Obaidka coota*. Instead of the *'s*, I add *ka* to the end of my name to show possession.

NOUNS

A *plural possessive noun* shows ownership by more than one person or thing. To form the possessive of a plural noun that ends in *s*, add an apostrophe (').

Two *boys'* backpacks were left behind.

The *stars'* patterns were beautiful that night.

We saw many *animals'* tracks as we hiked.

Exercise 14

Find the possessive noun in each sentence. Tell whether it is singular or plural.

1. The twins' great-grandfather had been a cowboy in Kansas.
2. Many of America's cowboys were African Americans.
3. The sisters wanted to learn about their family's history.
4. The sisters' plan was exciting.
5. Their grandparents' ranch was still there.
6. The trip was the girls' first visit to South Dakota.

For additional practice, turn to pages 196–197.

PRONOUNS

PRONOUN

A *pronoun* is a word that takes the place of one or more nouns.

Little Elk had a gift for painting.
He had a gift.
> He *takes the place of* Little Elk.

The warriors admired Little Elk.
They admired Little Elk.
> They *takes the place of* the warriors.

Exercise 15

Read each pair of sentences. Find the pronoun in the second sentence. Tell which word or words from the first sentence it replaces.

1. Little Elk loved to look at clouds.
   He felt joy from studying the sky.
2. Sometimes Little Elk's mother worried.
   She knew Little Elk was different.
3. One day Little Elk found some soil.
   He mixed the soil with rain water.
4. Little Elk later made a blue paint.
   It was the color of the sky.

For additional practice, turn to pages 198–199.

Writing Application

Write more sentences about Little Elk. Use some pronouns.

PRONOUNS

SINGULAR PRONOUN

A *singular pronoun* replaces a singular noun. The words *I*, *me*, *you*, *he*, *she*, *him*, *her*, and *it* are singular pronouns. Always capitalize the pronoun *I*.

Jorge, have *you* ever seen picture writing?
> You *stands for* Jorge.

Long ago, Native American peoples used *it* to communicate.
> It *stands for* picture writing.

***I* learned about picture writing from my grandfather.**
> I *replaces the speaker's name*.

***He* studied *it* in Arizona.**
> He *stands for* my grandfather. It *replaces* picture writing.

Exercise 16

Read each pair of sentences. Find the pronoun in the second sentence. Tell what word or words it replaces.

1. <u>Ramona</u>, look at the picture on the wall. Can <u>you</u> tell what the picture shows?
2. Look at this <u>picture</u>. <u>It</u> shows a boat.
3. <u>Grandmother</u> uses different pictures in her weaving. <u>She</u> weaves pictures of buffalo.
4. What does <u>Grandfather</u> show in his painting? <u>He</u> shows a village.
5. How do <u>Grandmother and Grandfather</u> show mountains? <u>They</u> use zigzags to show peaks and valleys.

For additional practice, turn to pages 200–201.

For additional practice, turn to pages 200–201.

Writing Application

Write sentences about the kinds of hobbies you enjoy. Use some pronouns.

PRONOUNS

PLURAL PRONOUN

A *plural pronoun* replaces a plural noun. The words *we, you, they, us,* and *them* are plural pronouns.

People use colors in many ways.
They use colors in many ways.
> They *replaces* people.

Artists use *colors* in paintings.
Artists use *them* in paintings.
> Them *replaces* colors.

Exercise 17

Revise each sentence. Replace each underlined word or group of words with a plural pronoun.

1. <u>My dad and I</u> like the work of early American artists.
2. My dad knows a lot about <u>many early American artists</u>.
3. <u>Early American painters</u> sometimes painted on wooden boards.
4. They made <u>paints</u> from plants and rocks.
5. Brown and red paints came from <u>roots</u>.
6. Other colors were made from <u>berries</u>.
7. Furniture making is also very interesting to <u>Dad and me</u>.
8. <u>Colonial furniture makers</u> took years to learn this craft.
9. <u>A master and a student</u> often worked together.
10. <u>My classmates and I</u> visited the exhibits in Williamsburg, Virginia.

For additional practice, turn to pages 202–203.

For additional practice, turn to pages 202–203.

PRONOUNS

A *subject pronoun* takes the place of one or more nouns in the subject of a sentence. The words *I, you, he, she, it, we,* and *they* are subject pronouns.

Mrs. Eldred is a talented person.
***She* always tries hard at new things.**
> She *replaces* Mrs. Eldred.

Mr. and Mrs. Eldred bought an easel.
***They* set it up in the yard.**
> They *replaces* Mr. and Mrs. Eldred.

The easel soon attracted the neighbors.
***It* was always surrounded by people.**
> It *replaces* the easel.

Exercise 18

Complete the second sentence in each pair. Tell which subject pronoun takes the place of the underlined word or words.

1. <u>Mrs. Eldred</u> sat in her chair.

   _____ painted circles, triangles, and squares.

2. <u>The paintings</u> were large and lively.

   _____ made people smile.

3. <u>Mr. Eldred</u> was surprised.

   "_____ didn't know you had such talent," he said.

4. Soon <u>the Eldreds</u> needed more room for all the paintings.

   _____ had nowhere to sit.

5. "<u>You and I</u> must do something about this," Mrs. Eldred said.

   "_____ can sell the paintings!" Mr. Eldred exclaimed.

For additional practice, turn to pages 204–205.

Writing Application

Describe a picture you like. Use subject pronouns in some of your sentences.

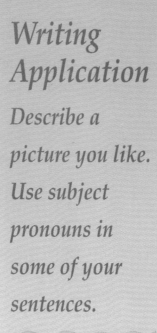
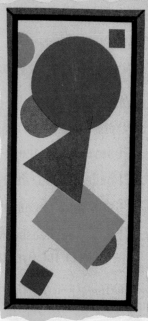

PRONOUNS

An *object pronoun* follows an action verb, such as *see* or *tell*, or a word such as *about, at, for, from, near, of, to,* and *with.* The words *me, you, him, her, it, us,* and *them* are object pronouns.

Detective Fox must solve a mystery.
Chef Rat will help *him* solve *it*.

> *Him* stands for Detective Fox.
> *It* stands for a mystery.

"I can't find my prize cheeses!"
cried Chef Rat.
"I have looked for *them* everywhere."

> *Them* stands for my prize cheeses.

Exercise 19

Choose the correct pronoun in parentheses ( ).

1. Mouse talked to the detective. She told (he/him) everything.
2. "I never took (they/them)," Mouse cried.
3. "I believe (you/they)," said Detective Fox.
4. "Bring (me/I) your menu," said Detective Fox.
5. "Pizza and cheesecake?" he laughed. "This is the answer for (we/us)."

For additional practice, turn to pages 206–207.

KIDS ON LANGUAGE

Hi. My name is Ha Ngoc Le [hä nôk lā], and I speak Vietnamese as well as English. Let me explain how to use pronouns in Vietnamese, and you'll understand something about my culture. In Vietnamese, there are pronouns that tell whether someone is a parent, a teacher, a friend, an older sister or brother, a child, and so on.

When I speak to my father, I use his title, *ba,* rather than the pronoun *you. Ba* means "father." It also means "someone very important."

If I were to give my father a book, I'd say, "Thuà ba con biêú ba cuôń sách naȳ." *Thuà* means "with great respect." The sentence translates, "With great respect, Father, I am giving Father this book."

115
GRAMMAR

ADJECTIVES

An *adjective* is a word that describes a noun. An adjective can come before the noun it describes. It can also follow a verb such as *is* or *seems*.

Two climbers pass Russell.

They carry *shiny* compasses.

Russell is *skillful*.

He throws *long* ropes and quickly travels up.

His *new red* poncho looks *tiny* from here.

Writing
Application

Use adjectives
to describe an
exciting
adventure you
have had.

Exercise 20

Find the adjectives in these sentences. Tell which nouns they describe.

1. Yosemite is beautiful.
2. Outside of Yosemite is flat desert.
3. Yosemite has tall cliffs.
4. Views are incredible!
5. One giant rock was carved in two pieces by ice.
6. It is made of hard gray rock called granite.
7. This rock's steep face is difficult to climb.
8. Climbers need special tools.
9. Many climbers find that it is hard work.
10. Old and young people enjoy climbing.

For additional practice, turn to pages 208–209.

ADJECTIVES

Some adjectives tell *how many.* Not all adjectives that tell how many give an exact number.

Many mysteries are found in nature.

Some mushrooms glow in the dark.

A tortoise can live for *one hundred* years!

The cheetah can run more than *seventy* miles an hour.

A dog named Laika was the *first* animal to orbit the earth.

Exercise 21

Find the adjective in each sentence that tells *how many*. Tell the noun it describes.

MYSTERY ANIMAL 1

1. This animal can be six feet in height.
2. It hops on two legs.
3. It lives wild on one continent.

MYSTERY ANIMAL 2

4. This shy sea creature has eight arms.
5. It has three hearts.
6. The female lays many eggs at once.

For additional practice, turn to pages 210–211.

Writing Application

Write three clues about a mystery animal. Use adjectives that tell how many.

ADJECTIVES

ADJECTIVES THAT TELL *WHAT KIND*

Some adjectives tell *what kind*. They can describe size, shape, or color. They can help you know how something looks, sounds, feels, tastes, or smells.

A *tall* woman stands on the corner.

She wears a *red* hat.

This *quiet* detective is Madame Girard.

Tiny cameras are hidden in her hat.

Exercise 22

In each sentence, find the adjective that tells *what kind*. Tell what noun it describes.

1. Madame Girard also uses tiny computers.
2. She keeps them in her secret pouch.
3. She takes careful notes on her cases.
4. Notes help her solve difficult mysteries.
5. She once found lost diamonds.
6. Yesterday she found Lulu's famous parrot.
7. "I find hidden things," she brags.
8. Good detectives, though, sometimes need help.
9. Today Madame Girard lost an important key.
10. Lulu helped her embarrassed friend find it.

For additional practice, turn to pages 212–213.

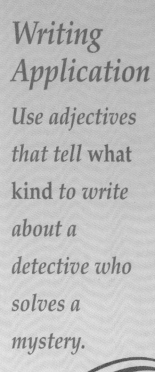

Writing Application

Use adjectives that tell what kind *to write about a detective who solves a mystery.*

121

ADJECTIVES

ARTICLES

The adjectives *a, an,* and *the* are called **articles.** Use *a* before a word that begins with a consonant sound. Use *an* before a word that begins with a vowel sound. Use *the* before a word that begins with a consonant or a vowel.

Have you ever seen *an* owl?
> *The article* an *comes before* owl *because* owl *begins with the vowel* o.

The owl is *a* nocturnal animal.
> *The article* a *comes before* nocturnal *because* nocturnal *begins with a consonant.*

Nocturnal animals sleep during *the* day.
The owl is active at night.
> *The article* the *can be used before a word that begins with a consonant or a vowel.*

Exercise 23

Choose the article in parentheses ( ) that correctly completes each sentence.

1. Where could you go to find (a/an) owl?
2. That depends on (an/the) kind of owl you are looking for.
3. You might find a barn owl's nest in (an/a) old building.
4. The snowy owl lives in (the/an) cold North.
5. In Mexico you might see (an/a) elf owl.
6. The burrowing owl makes its home in (an/a) hole in the ground.
7. When is (an/the) best time to go owling?
8. You usually cannot see owls during (the/an) day.
9. Late at night is (an/a) perfect time.
10. Wear (an/a) warm coat on your owl search.

For additional practice, turn to pages 214–215.

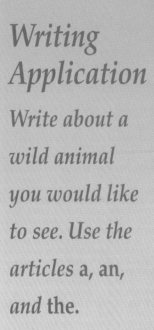

Writing Application

Write about a wild animal you would like to see. Use the articles a, an, *and* the.

ADJECTIVES

Adjectives can describe by *comparing* people, animals, places, or things. Add *-er* to most adjectives to compare two things.

My father is *taller* than me.

This stream is *shallower* than that one.

Add *-est* to most adjectives to compare more than two things.

Is the pine the *tallest* tree of all?

This is the *deepest* river in the world.

Exercise 24

Tell whether to add *-er* or *-est* to each underlined adjective.

1. A raccoon's front feet are <u>small</u> than its back feet.
2. A large animal leaves <u>deep</u> prints than a small animal.
3. A grizzly bear's footprints are the <u>deep</u> of any I have seen.
4. The badger has <u>long</u> claws than the fox.
5. The badger has the <u>long</u> claws of any animal its size.
6. A mouse made the <u>small</u> animal tracks of all on this trail.
7. The riverbank is <u>steep</u> over here than over there.
8. Animal tracks are <u>clear</u> in wet places than in dry ones.
9. Find the <u>damp</u> spot of all, and look for tracks.
10. Is this marsh the <u>large</u> one in all of Minnesota?

For additional practice, turn to pages 216–217.

Writing Application

Imagine that you have found a huge animal track. Use -er and -est to help describe its size.

GRAMMAR

ADJECTIVES

ADJECTIVES THAT COMPARE: MORE, MOST

Some adjectives need the word *more* or *most* for comparing. Use *more* with an adjective to compare two things.

Parrots are *more* talkative than parakeets. Some people think parrots are *more* intelligent, too.

Use *most* with an adjective to compare more than two things.

In Ms. Soare's pet shop, the *most* talkative bird of all is the mynah bird.

Exercise 25

Complete each sentence with *more* or *most*.

1. The quetzal is the _____ beautiful bird in all Central America.
2. Its feathers are _____ colorful than a parakeet's feathers.
3. Its tail is the _____ splendid of any bird in the rain forest.
4. Wild avocados are the _____ important food of all in its diet.

For additional practice, turn to pages 218–219.

126

GRAMMAR

LANGUAGE FEATURE:
ADJECTIVES THAT COMPARE

Hi. My name is Andrew Santisteban [sän•tēs´tā•vän], and my family is from Cuba. It is very important for me to know Spanish. My grandmother Raquel speaks only Spanish. If I want to talk to her, I must speak Spanish so that she can understand me.

In Spanish, when we compare one thing with another, we do not use a different adjective. We use the word *más* with the adjective to make the comparison. Here is an example:

Este libro es *grande.* (This book is big.)

Este libro es *más grande* que ese libro. (This book is bigger than that book.)

Este libro es el *más grande* de todos los libros. (This book is the biggest of all the books.)

VERBS

VERB

A *verb* is a word that shows action. A verb is the main word in the predicate of a sentence. A verb and its subject should agree.

Frogs *live* the first part of their lives as water animals.

They *spend* the rest of their lives as land animals.

All frogs *begin* their lives as tadpoles.

Tadpoles *look* like little fish.

Exercise 26

Tell what the verb is in each sentence.

1. Tadpoles begin their lives underwater.
2. A tadpole's body changes over time.
3. Its tail grows long.
4. The back legs kick.
5. Next, the front legs develop.
6. Tadpoles breathe through gills.
7. An older tadpole loses its gills and its tail.
8. The change becomes complete.
9. A tiny frog climbs onto land.
10. The new frog appears as a land animal.

For additional practice, turn to pages 220–221.

For additional practice, turn to pages 220–221.

Writing Application

Describe a frog. Circle the verbs you use.

VERBS

An *action verb* is a word that tells what the subject of a sentence does.

Most frogs *live* near water.

Tree frogs *make* their home in trees.

A frog *catches* insects with its sticky tongue.

It *jumps* high and far.

Some frogs *leap* twenty times the length of their bodies!

Exercise 27

Read each sentence. Tell the action verb.

1. My family attended an unusual contest.
2. Hundreds of frog owners enter the Jumping Frog Jubilee.
3. Each owner sets a frog down in the middle of a circle.
4. The owner makes a lot of noise.
5. A good frog leaps very far.
6. The judges measure the leap carefully.
7. My frog, Hugo, sat inside his circle.
8. I clapped my hands.
9. The next day I took Hugo back to his stream.
10. He hopped far out into the water.

For additional practice, turn to pages 222–223.

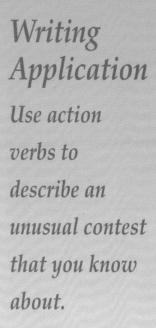

Writing Application

Use action verbs to describe an unusual contest that you know about.

VERBS

Sometimes the predicate has two or more verbs. The *main verb* is the most important verb in a sentence.

One type of bird <u>has</u> *become* an excellent swimmer.

That penguin <u>had</u> *dived* many times to the ocean floor.

Some birds <u>have</u> *run* very fast.

Exercise 28

Tell the main verb in each sentence.

1. That squirrel has floated through the air!
2. It has landed safely in a tree.
3. Juan has disappeared inside the house.
4. He had passed his video camera to me.
5. We have taped some amazing animals.
6. This flying squirrel had played a starring role.
7. Have you noticed this picture?
8. The squirrel's body has changed into a glider.
9. It had soared from tree to tree.
10. We have waited for the squirrel's next flight.

For additional practice, turn to pages 224–225.

Writing Application

Write about an animal that flies. Circle the main verbs you use.

VERBS

A *helping verb* can work with the main verb to tell about an action. The helping verb always comes before the main verb. The words *have, has,* and *had* are often used as helping verbs.

My dad *had* studied all kinds of flight.

I *have* learned a lot from him.

We *have* gone on a balloon flight together.

Now I *have* become a fan of his!

Exercise 29

In each sentence, tell which word is the helping verb.

1. My dad has owned many types of flying machines.
2. We have traveled in most of them together.
3. We had soared over the land in hot-air balloons and gliders.
4. We have wanted a very special plane.
5. I had looked at pictures of this plane in history books.
6. Our plane has finally landed at the town airport!
7. We have replaced many of its parts.
8. Dad had painted it.
9. People have called us from all over the country.
10. Dad has planned a party in honor of the special old plane.

For additional practice, turn to pages 226–227.

For additional practice, turn to pages 226–227.

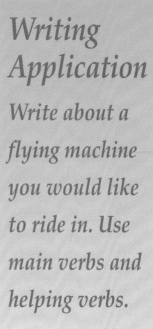

Writing Application

Write about a flying machine you would like to ride in. Use main verbs and helping verbs.

VERBS

The *tense* of a verb shows when the action happens.

PRESENT-TIME VERB

A *present-time verb* tells about action that happens now. The correct form of the verb depends on the subject of the sentence. Add *s* or *es* to most present-time verbs when the subject of the sentence is *he, she, it,* or a singular noun.

A seal *sleeps* near the edge of the ice.

Another seal *splashes* in the water near her.

Do not add *s* or *es* to a present-time verb when the subject is *I, you,* or a plural noun.

I *watch* them silently.

You always *talk* too loudly on our hikes.

Exercise 30

Choose the correct present-time verb in parentheses ( ).

1. Two scientists (search/searches) the ice for seals.
2. The man (use/uses) field glasses.
3. The woman (see/sees) two mother seals and their babies.
4. The seals (sleep/sleeps) in the warm sun.
5. The man eagerly (take/takes) out his camera.
6. His movement (alarm/alarms) the seals.
7. The scientists (arrives/arrive) too late.
8. The baby seals (dives/dive) into a hole in the ice.
9. The mother seals (follow/follows).
10. The two people (sit/sits) down to wait.

For additional practice, turn to pages 228–229.

Writing Application

Use present-time verbs to write a story about an animal's secret hiding place.

VERBS

A *past-time verb* shows that an action happened in the past. Add *ed* or *d* to most present-time verbs to make them show past time.

In 1993 it *rained* for many weeks.

People *piled* sandbags along the bank of the river.

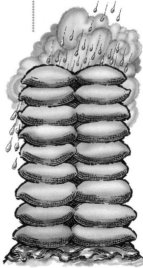

Exercise 31

Tell which verb in parentheses ( ) correctly completes each sentence so that the action is in the past.

1. The Missouri River (swelled/swell) with rain.
2. People (fear/feared) that the river would flood.
3. After weeks of rain, the Mississippi River (spilled/spill) over its banks.
4. The two mighty rivers (flowed/flow) together then.
5. Farmland (turned/turn) into lake bottoms.
6. Animals (rush/rushed) for higher ground.
7. The flood (lasted/last) for weeks.
8. When it was over, people (returned/return) to their homes.

For additional practice, turn to pages 230–231.

KIDS ON LANGUAGE

Hello! My name is Servincy Edmond [sûr´vin•sē əd•môŋ´], and my family comes from Haiti. I speak both Creole and English. Creole is a combination of French, Spanish, and other languages. Most of the time, I speak Creole at home because that is what my parents speak.

Creole uses verbs a little differently than English does. In English, the spelling of the verb often changes to tell the present, past, or future. In Creole, the spelling of the verb stays the same. Short words are added to a sentence to tell the tense.

Here is an example. The verb in the sentences below is *manjé*. Notice how it does not change.

M <u>ap</u> manjé.   (I am eating.)

Mouen <u>té</u> manjé.   (I have eaten.)

M <u>a</u> manjé.   (I will eat.)

139
GRAMMAR

VERBS

An *irregular verb* is a verb that does not end with *ed* to show past time. This chart shows some irregular verbs.

Present	Past	Past with Helping Verb
come, comes	came	(have, has, had) come
do, does	did	(have, has, had) done
drive, drives	drove	(have, has, had) driven
eat, eats	ate	(have, has, had) eaten
give, gives	gave	(have, has, had) given
go, goes	went	(have, has, had) gone

My family and I *drove* across the state of Washington.

We *came* to a stop at Mount Saint Helens.

None of us *had seen* a volcano before.

Exercise 32

Choose the correct verb in parentheses ( ) to complete each sentence.

1. We had (drives/driven) for hours.
2. We (came/comes) to a picnic area in a little valley.
3. "Let's (eat/ate)!" we cried.
4. We (ate/eats) lunch at the base of Mount Saint Helens.
5. Mom (go/went) to get her guidebook.
6. People (drove/driven) away fast when the volcano erupted in 1980.
7. After the eruption, many (come, came) back to rebuild.
8. We discovered that the eruption of Mount Saint Helens (do/did) things to help the ecosystem.
9. The volcano (gave/given) nutrients back to the soil.
10. I want to (went/go) back one day.

For additional practice, turn to pages 232–233.

Writing Application

Use irregular verbs to write about an amazing natural event.

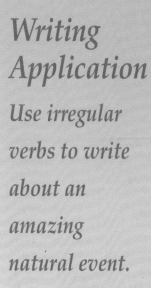

VERBS

Here are more irregular verbs. See how these
verbs are used in the sentences below.

Present	Past	Past with Helping Verb
have, has	had	(have, has, had) had
ride, rides	rode	(have, has, had) ridden
run, runs	ran	(have, has, had) run
say, says	said	(have, has, had) said
see, sees	saw	(have, has, had) seen
take, takes	took	(have, has, had) taken
think, thinks	thought	(have, has, had) thought

Last night, we *saw* Aunt Louise.

She *thought* a wolf had been around.

She *said* she would make up a story about it.

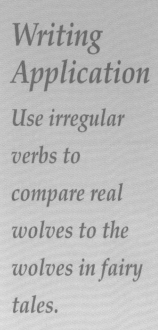

Exercise 33

Choose the correct verb in parentheses ( ) to complete each sentence.

1. A plump pig (saw/seen) the wolf coming closer.
2. At first, he (ran/run) away from his enemy.
3. Then he (saw/seen) an apple tree.
4. The pig (thinked/thought) of a cunning plan.
5. He (say/said) to himself, "I will climb to the highest branch."
6. The pig (taked/took) the largest, reddest apple he could find and dropped it.
7. The wolf (run/ran) after the apple.
8. By that time, the pig had (ran/run) safely home.

For additional practice, turn to pages 234–235.

For additional practice, turn to pages 234–235.

Writing Application

Use irregular verbs to compare real wolves to the wolves in fairy tales.

VERBS

Forms of the verb *be* link the subject of the
sentence to one or more words in the
predicate. They tell what or where
someone or something is or was. The
subject and the form of the verb *be*
should agree. This chart shows some of
the forms of the verb *be*:

Pronoun	Present Time	Past Time
I	am	was
you	are	were
he, she, it	is	was
we	are	were
you	are	were
they	are	were

Anna *is* a clever girl.

She *was* the winner of the Young
Secret Agent Award.

We *are* proud of her.

Exercise 34

Use your wits to solve the mystery below. First, choose the correct form of the verb *be* to complete each sentence. Then when you have completed items 1–10, tell what you think happened.

1. Madame Monique (is/are) in the penthouse.
2. She and Miss Agatha (is/are) the only ones there.
3. An uninvited guest (was/were) there just a minute ago!
4. Their dog, Bruno, (were/was) outside at the time with the chauffeur.
5. "I (am/is) worried!" Madame Monique cries.
6. The clues (are/is) in plain sight.
7. Some orange fur (is/are) on the window ledge.
8. All the fish in the fish tank (are/is) gone.
9. Miss Agatha's cup of milk (is/are) empty, but her cookies are still there.
10. Four small paw prints (are/is) on the floor.

What do *you* think happened?

For additional practice, turn to pages 236–237.

For additional practice, turn to pages 236–237.

Writing Application

Use forms of the verb be *to write a short mystery story.*

ADVERBS

ADVERB

An *adverb* is a word that describes a verb. An adverb may tell *where, when,* or *how* an action happens.

Today we visited a railroad museum. **WHEN**

My brother and I raced *eagerly* toward the railroad cars. **HOW**

We ran *ahead,* and our parents followed. **WHERE**

Exercise 35

Find the adverb in each sentence. Tell whether it says *where, when,* or *how* the action happens.

1. First, we climbed on an old caboose.
2. André rang the bell loudly.
3. An engineer stood nearby.
4. He patiently answered our questions.
5. Next, we visited an antique train.
6. André sat on a faded seat, and I stood outside.

For additional practice, turn to pages 238–239.

LANGUAGE FEATURE: ADVERBS

My name is Amy Kalonaheskie [ā′mē kä′lon•ə•hes′kē], and I attend school in Cherokee, North Carolina. I have been learning Cherokee since before I started kindergarten.

In Cherokee, verbs do more than tell an action. They can tell *when* something happens and also *how* or *where* it happens. For example, we use a verb that means "something is moving." I add the syllable *wi-* before the verb. This changes its meaning to "something is moving far away."

I speak Cherokee with my grandmother at home and when I greet friends in school. Everyone in my school learns Cherokee. We learn the Cherokee alphabet, which has eighty-six letters. We also learn words. My class will be writing stories in Cherokee later this year.

TO, TOO, TWO

Use *to* when you mean "in the direction of."

I am going *to* a vaudeville show.

Use *too* when you mean "also."

My family is going, *too*.

Use *two* when you mean the number.

Each ticket costs *two* dollars.

Exercise 36

Complete each sentence by telling whether to use *to, too,* or *two.*

1. We went _____ the theater.
2. The mayor came, _____.
3. An usher showed us _____ our seats.
4. "Welcome _____ the best show ever!" an announcer said.
5. The first _____ performers did a number of good tricks.
6. They sang songs, _____.
7. Then _____ actors told some funny jokes.
8. I had never been _____ a vaudeville show before.
9. There were _____ songs in the finale.
10. "I know this song and the last one, _____!" the mayor said.

For additional practice, turn to pages 240–241.

Writing Application

Use to, too, *and* two *to write about a performance you have seen.*

YOUR, YOU'RE

Use *your* when you mean "belonging to you."

Grandpa, do you have *your* ice skates?

Use *you're* when you mean "you are."

Eric, *you're* going to be amazed at how much fun this is.

Exercise 37

Read this conversation. Tell whether *your* or *you're* should be used to complete each sentence. Explain your choice.

1. _____ my best pupil, Eric.
2. Pull _____ laces tight.
3. Now _____ ready to skate safely.
4. Were _____ legs this wobbly when you started, Grandpa?
5. Yes, but _____ getting better, Eric.
6. _____ skates flash like silver.
7. _____ saying I'm a fast skater?
8. What was _____ greatest race, Grandpa?
9. I won a medal once, but _____ too young to remember that.
10. Grandpa, _____ the best skater I know.

For additional practice, turn to pages 242–243.

TROUBLESOME WORDS

ITS, IT'S

Use *its* when you mean "belonging to it."

The pyramid is huge. We look up at *its* steep sides.

Explorers have found *its* seven sunken chambers.

Use *it's* when you mean "it is."

It's fun to explore.

I think *it's* a great place to visit.

Exercise 38

Use *its* or *it's* to complete the sentences.

1. What is that? _____ a mummy!
2. _____ thousands of years old.
3. _____ wrapped tightly in strips of cloth.
4. The inner chamber of the pyramid is large. Ancient drawings cover _____ walls.
5. In one picture, a dog follows _____ owner.
6. _____ teeth are long and sharp.
7. Look at this mask. _____ made of solid gold!
8. _____ important to keep careful records.
9. Photograph each item, and write down _____ exact location.
10. _____ a job that is certain to take many weeks.

For additional practice, turn to pages 244–245.

Writing Application

Write a story about finding treasure. Use its *and* it's *correctly.*

THEIR, THERE, THEY'RE

Use *their* when you mean "belonging to them."

Pirates sailed *their* galleons.

Use *there* when you mean "in that place."

The captain hid his riches in the trunk over *there*.

Use *they're* when you mean "they are."

***They're* the most incredible jewels I have ever seen.**

Exercise 39

Complete each sentence. Tell whether to use *their, there,* or *they're.*

1. Pirates sailed _____ ships to islands in the Caribbean.
2. Royal ships from England, France, and Spain sailed _____, too.
3. Pirates filled _____ galleons with riches from these ships.
4. _____ ships sometimes sank during storms.
5. Are those ships still _____ at the bottom of the sea?
6. _____ hard to find.
7. _____ rich cargo attracts divers.
8. _____ still interesting to study today.

For additional practice, turn to pages 246–247.

For additional practice, turn to pages 246–247.

Writing Application

Write a story about a hidden treasure. Use their, there, *and* they're *correctly.*

155

USAGE

COMMAS

Use a **comma (,)** to set off the words *yes, no,* and *well* at the beginning of a sentence.

Well, that was a strange place.

Yes, it was the most ominous place I've ever been.

Well, should we visit another fun house?

No, I don't think so.

Exercise 40

Read these sentences. Tell where to put the comma.

1. Are you having trouble walking? Yes I am!
2. Is the floor a little slanted? Well it must be.
3. No the walls aren't straight!
4. Well now we know why this place seems so strange.
5. No I don't think we do. Look at that bunny!
6. No that's not a bunny. That's just a shadow.
7. Yes you're right. Did it fool you?
8. No of course not. I know all about fun houses.

For additional practice, turn to pages 248–249.

Kids on Language

Hello! My name is Asuka Eguchi [äz′kə e•gōō′chē]. I was born in Japan and lived there until I was five. My parents tell me that my name in Japanese means "I have a bright future."

Japanese is a very interesting language. In writing, it has more than 1,000 characters. Also, in Japanese there are no exact expressions for the words *yes* and *no*.

For example, to answer the question "Do you want to go?" a person would not answer, "Yes, I want to go" or "No, I don't want to go." The person would answer, "I want to go" or "I don't want to go."

COMMAS

Use a *comma* (,) after each item except the last one in a series of three or more items.

The desert is hot, dry, and sandy.

Snakes, lizards, and tortoises live there.

Sometimes the wind will blow, swirl, or whip the sand around.

Exercise 41

Tell where commas belong in each sentence.

1. The desert seems to shimmer shine and bubble in the hot sun.
2. Imaginary sights can appear to people when they are tired thirsty and hot.
3. A person might see a cool pond a green forest or a blue swimming pool.
4. These people should shake their heads rub their eyes and drink some water.
5. Then the mirage will flicker fade and disappear.

For additional practice, turn to pages 250–251.

Handwriting

Handwriting

Handwriting Tips

Using correct posture, writing grip, and paper position can help you write clearly. These tips will help you get ready for writing. See pages 161–168 for tips to help you form letters and words.

Posture

- Sit up straight with both feet on the floor. Your hips should be toward the back of the chair.

- Lean forward slightly, but don't slouch.

Paper Position

- Slant the paper toward the elbow of your writing arm. Hold the top corner of the paper with your other hand.

Writing Grip

- Hold your pen or pencil about an inch from the point.

- Hold it between your thumb and pointer finger. Rest it on your middle finger. Let your other fingers curve under.

Left-hander

Right-hander

Uppercase and Lowercase Manuscript Alphabet

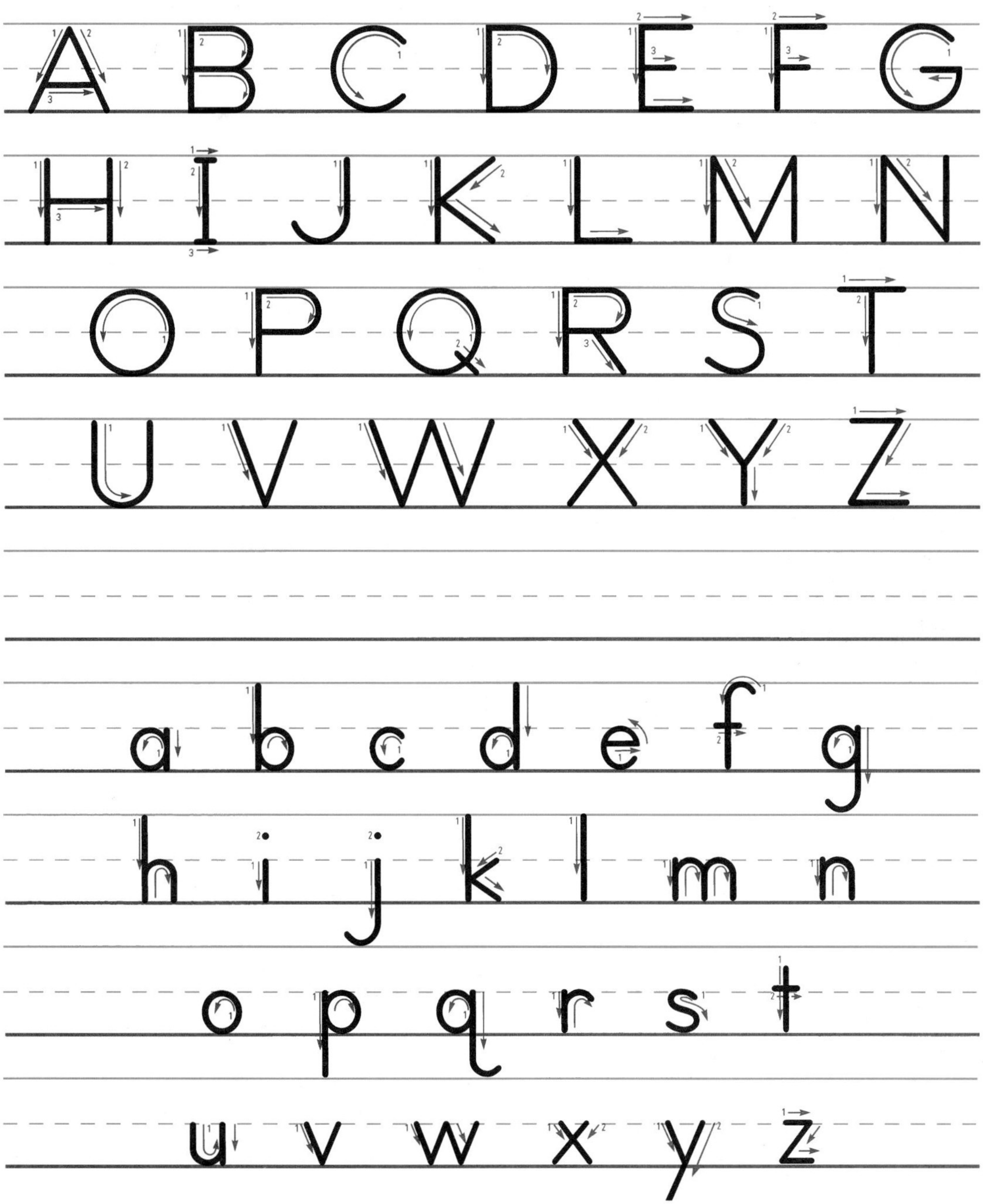
A B C D E F G
H I J K L M N
O P Q R S T
U V W X Y Z
a b c d e f g
h i j k l m n
o p q r s t
u v w x y z

Handwriting

A B C D E F G

H I J K L M N

O P Q R S T

U V W X Y Z

a b c d e f g

h i j k l m n

o p q r s t

u v w x y z

Elements of Handwriting

Shape

Make each letter the correct shape.

correct   **incorrect**

Tuesday   *Tuesday*

Spacing

Leave the correct amount of space between letters.

Leave one pencil space between words and after end punctuation.

We ate pears.

Position

Write all letters so they sit on the bottom line.

correct

coat

incorrect

coat

Size

Tall letters touch both the top line and the bottom line.

The tails on all letters touch the descender line.

Short letters touch the midline and the bottom line.

correct

pull

incorrect

pull

Slant

Slant your letters in the same direction. If you slant your paper
correctly, it will help you slant your letters.

correct　　　　　　　　　　　　　　　　**incorrect**

kite　　　　　　　*kite*

Stroke

When you write, keep your letter strokes smooth and even.
The letters should not be too light or too dark.

correct　　　　　　　**too light**　　　　　　**too dark**

car　　　*car*　　　*car*

165

HANDWRITING

Joining Letters

Use an overcurve stroke when you join another letter to a circle stroke letter. You will have to retrace the circle stroke.

ra ed ma ic ng

Look at the way these letters join with undercurve and overcurve letters.

undercurve

sl fe tr

overcurve

un im

Look at the way the uppercase letters **J**, **Y**, and **Z** join with lowercase letters.

undercurve

Je Ye Ze

overcurve

Jo Ya

Look at the way these letters join.

Ca Hi Ko Re Ur

incorrect   correct

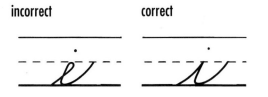

Do not loop **i**.
The **i** could look like **e**.

incorrect   correct

Touch the top line.
The **l** could look like **e**.

incorrect   correct

Be sure the slant stroke returns to the bottom line. The **u** could look like **v**.

incorrect   correct

Loop left.
The **g** could look like **q**.

incorrect   correct

Start at the top line.
The **N** could look like lowercase **n**.

incorrect   correct

Close the circle along the top line and do not loop. The **A** could look like **Cl**.

incorrect   correct

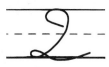

Start at the midline and undercurve to the top line. The **L** could look like **Q**.

incorrect   correct

Remember that **P** does not join with other letters. The **P** could look like **R**.

incorrect   correct

Remember that **V** has no joining stroke. The **V** could look like **U**.

ADDITIONAL PRACTICE

A. Read each group of words. Write whether each group of words is a sentence.

Examples:

Spiders are fun to watch.

sentence

Big and hairy with eight legs.

not a sentence

1. Mrs. Bentley has a special hobby.
2. She raises spiders.
3. Tarantulas are relatives of the spiders in your garden.
4. Are quiet pets!
5. Mrs. Bentley takes good care of her collection.
6. Some people think they are scary creatures!
7. Can live for thirty years.
8. One tarantula sheds its skin.
9. Crawls on her arm.
10. It does not bite her.

B. Identify each sentence. Revise each of the other groups of words so it becomes a sentence.

Example:

Peppers in Victor's garden.

Victor grows peppers in his garden.

11. Victor's mother makes delicious salsa.
12. Hot peppers, tomatoes, and onions.
13. Victor planted pepper seeds in January.
14. In milk cartons filled with soil.
15. He watered the seeds each day.
16. Saw sprouts in the carton.
17. Inside his house for weeks.
18. He planted little plants outside.
19. Pepper plants like warm weather.
20. Protected the plants from snails.
21. Victor watered the plants every day.
22. Ripe red peppers!
23. He washed them and chopped them up.
24. Delicious in tacos and on nachos!
25. Winner of the blue ribbon at the fair!

STATEMENTS AND QUESTIONS

A. Read the sentences. Identify each statement.

Example:

Lester travels with his parents.

   statement

1. He has lived in eight countries.
2. Do you know where Rwanda is?
3. Isn't that country in east Africa?
4. Lester's family lived there for years.
5. The family lived in Japan last year.

B. Read the sentences. Identify each question.

Example:

Do you know anyone who has lived in a different country?

   question

6. Where does Lester live now?
7. He and his family moved to Canada.
8. Isn't Vancouver a beautiful city?
9. Does Lester study Japanese in school?
10. He studies the Japanese system of writing called *kanji.*

C. Read each sentence. Write whether it is a statement or a question. Revise each question to make it a statement.

Example:

Wasn't Elizabeth Cochrane a famous writer?

question—Elizabeth Cochrane was a famous writer.

11. She was a brave newspaper reporter.
12. Was she born in 1867?
13. Didn't she use the name Nellie Bly?
14. Were women treated poorly in jails then?
15. Cochrane went to jail to find out.
16. Did she write about what happened?
17. Were people shocked by her articles?
18. After that, the jails treated women better.
19. Was Cochrane famous by the time she was twenty-one?
20. Did she decide to travel around the world?
21. Jules Verne wrote a book about world travel.
22. Cochrane wanted to circle the globe, too.
23. Had airplanes already been invented?
24. Cochrane left New York on November 14, 1889.
25. It took her only seventy-three days to travel around the world.

EXCLAMATIONS AND COMMANDS

A. Read the sentences. Write which ones are exclamations.

Example:

What a special flower the dandelion is!

exclamation

1. This is a tasty salad!
2. What are these green leaves called?
3. What a surprise this is!
4. I've never eaten dandelion leaves before!
5. The young leaves are not bitter at all.

B. Read the sentences. Write which ones are commands.

Example:

Dig up the roots of those dandelions.

command

6. Give them to Grandma.
7. She will wash them and roast them.
8. Please grind up the roots.
9. Stay away from this boiling pot.
10. Give your mother this cup of tea.

PRACTICE

C. Read each sentence. Write whether it is an exclamation or a command.

Example:
This town smells funny!
  exclamation

11. Try a bit of my spaghetti.
12. How tasty it is!
13. I used a whole garlic in the pot of sauce!
14. Leave enough in the pot for my sister.
15. Find Gilroy on this map of California.
16. You've located the garlic capital!
17. Come with me to the Garlic Festival.
18. There must be ten thousand garlic plants!
19. Every food at this festival has garlic!
20. That stand is selling garlic ice cream!
21. I can't believe you're really eating it!
22. Give me a little taste.
23. Take the rest of the ice cream home.
24. What fun we've had at the festival!
25. Brush your teeth for a long time tonight.

PARTS OF A SENTENCE: SUBJECT

A. Read each sentence. Write the subject.

Example:

My brother loves apples.

My brother

1. These apples have a lovely yellow color.
2. The smell reminds him of honey.
3. Theo takes one to school every day.
4. His grandfather made an apple pie.
5. The whole family enjoyed that treat.
6. Elena prefers Northern Spy apples.
7. A large red apple sits on the sill.
8. The first bite will be the best.
9. The Green Nursery sells twenty-six kinds.
10. Each kind produces a different flavor.

B. Revise each group of words by adding a subject.

Example:

_____ has the most beautiful garden.
  Mrs. Gonzales has the most beautiful garden.

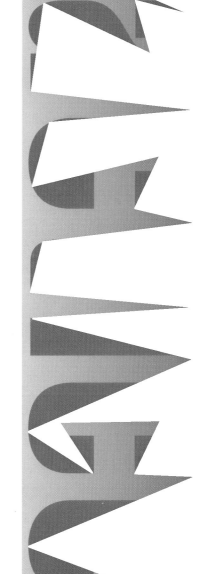

11. _____ has a tall tree in her yard.
12. _____ are the most delicious fruit.
13. _____ are the worst pests.
14. _____ build nests in tall trees.
15. _____ bloom early in the spring.
16. _____ is my favorite flavor of jelly.
17. _____ climb trees very fast.
18. _____ need water and sunshine.
19. _____ turn red in the fall.
20. _____ flies from flower to flower.
21. _____ have very sharp thorns.
22. _____ grows quickly.
23. _____ likes strawberries.
24. _____ chases cats all the time.
25. _____ is the best place for a picnic.

PARTS OF A SENTENCE: PREDICATE

A. Read the sentences. Write the predicate of each one.

Example:

The grocer filled a huge jar with peanuts.

filled a huge jar with peanuts

1. The local newspaper announced a contest.
2. Porter's Bicycle Shop sponsors the contest.
3. The store displays a jar in its window.
4. Each student guesses the number of peanuts in the jar.
5. Mina wants to win the grand prize very much.
6. Her brother needs a new bicycle.
7. This smart young woman estimates the size of the jar.
8. She measures some peanuts.
9. The jar can hold about 1,750 peanuts.
10. Mina's answer is closest to the correct number!

B. Write each sentence, and underline the predicate.

Example:

My aunt collects string.

  My aunt collects string.

11. She rolls her string into a ball.
12. My aunt ties a new piece of string to the last one on the ball.
13. Each piece makes the ball a little bigger.
14. My aunt's hobby is important to her.
15. People drop pieces of string in odd places.
16. She gathers string from many places.
17. A string ball grows slowly.
18. Francis A. Johnson started a ball of string in 1950.
19. He added to it for 28 years.
20. The ball was almost 13 feet tall by 1978.
21. This amazing ball was 40 feet around.
22. Mr. Johnson became the most famous string collector in the world.
23. The ball of string became famous, too.
24. It was the largest ball of string in history.
25. A hobby can make a person famous.

A. Read each sentence. Write the nouns.

Example:

My cousin is a pilot.

cousin, pilot

1. My best friend is a flier, too.
2. My pal flew over our house.
3. This amazing girl may fly to the moon one day!
4. The father is also a pilot.
5. This man owns a small plane.
6. The inside has only four seats.
7. The family decided to take a trip.
8. The aircraft had to stop for fuel.
9. The group reached an airport 3,000 miles away.
10. The passengers arrived safely.

B. Write the sentences. Underline the nouns.

Example:

The lake at our camp has an area where people can swim.

The <u>lake</u> at our <u>camp</u> has an <u>area</u> where <u>people</u> can swim.

11. The water is cold.
12. The boy stands on the dock.
13. A lifeguard stands nearby.
14. The child dives into the lake.
15. This young camper swims for ten minutes.
16. The counselor later shakes the hand of the swimmer.
17. This test was difficult.
18. Now this student can learn to use a canoe.
19. A paddle lies on the shore.
20. The team practices away from the rocks.
21. The man ties the boat to the dock with rope.

COMMON NOUNS

A. Read the sentences. Write the common nouns.

Example:

Levi Hutchins was a clockmaker.

clockmaker

1. This young person lived in Concord, New Hampshire.
2. Hutchins always started work early.
3. This fellow was awake before the sun came up.
4. Some people don't like to get up when the sky is dark.
5. Sometimes Hutchins was so tired he stayed in bed.
6. The man had an idea for a new kind of clock.
7. This machine would have a bell in it.
8. The owner would set the piece for a certain time.
9. A chime would ring then.
10. What invention did Hutchins create?

B. Revise each sentence. Replace the underlined common nouns with other common nouns. Your sentences may be silly.

Example:

The <u>platypus</u> is an unusual <u>animal</u>.

The kangaroo is an unusual creature.

11. The <u>platypus</u> lives in Australia and Tasmania.
12. It has thick <u>fur</u> on its <u>body</u>.
13. Its <u>beak</u> is like the <u>bill</u> of a <u>duck</u>.
14. Its <u>tail</u> is like that of a <u>beaver</u>.
15. <u>Platypuses</u> live in <u>rivers</u> and <u>lakes</u>.
16. They eat <u>worms</u>, <u>snails</u>, and <u>fish</u>.
17. <u>Platypuses</u> have <u>flippers</u> instead of <u>paws</u>.
18. These furry <u>animals</u> are good <u>swimmers</u>.
19. The <u>animal</u> has sharp <u>spurs</u> on its <u>ankles</u>.
20. It will strike at an <u>enemy</u> with these <u>spurs</u>.

PROPER NOUNS

A. The nouns in these sentences are underlined.
Write each proper noun.

Example:

Pompeii was an ancient city.

Pompeii

1. A terrible thing happened in Pompeii long ago.
2. The tragedy happened in August.
3. One afternoon, the people of Italy heard an explosion.
4. A volcano named Mount Vesuvius erupted!
5. A few citizens fled toward the Mediterranean Sea.
6. Red-hot lava flowed toward this city near Naples.
7. The town of Herculaneum was also in danger that day.
8. The Metropolitan Museum shows objects the residents used there.
9. Families in some parts of Europe still worry about volcanoes.
10. Mount Etna is also a mountain there.

B. Write the proper nouns in these sentences.

Example:

Many unusual animals are in the London Zoo.

London Zoo

11. London is the capital of England.

12. Its zoo is one of the largest in Europe.

13. In 1865 an elephant from Africa was brought to the zoo.

14. The elephant named Jumbo was sold to a man who owned a circus.

15. His name was P. T. Barnum.

16. Queen Victoria wanted the elephant to stay in the London Zoo.

17. Barnum brought the elephant to North America anyway.

18. People in New York, Chicago, and Philadelphia went to see this huge beast.

19. Americans began saying that anything large was "jumbo-sized."

20. Some large elephants have been found in Namibia recently.

SINGULAR AND PLURAL NOUNS

A. Write the singular noun or nouns in each sentence.

Example:

Laura sends her friend postcards.

Laura, friend

1. Sarah writes letters to her pal.
2. Her sister moved to a land across the sea.
3. She needs a coat and mittens there in the winter.
4. Laura lives with her parents near the beach.
5. On many days in January she wears shorts.

B. Write the plural noun or nouns in each sentence.

Example:

Florida has many miles of beaches.

miles, beaches

6. The two friends make bracelets.
7. These treasures are kept in painted boxes.
8. Sarah sends her favorite books to her friend.
9. Laura sends drawings of a costume.
10. Sarah laughs when she sees the shoes for this costume.

C. Look at the nouns in these sentences. If the underlined noun is singular, write its plural form. If it is plural, write its singular form.

Example:

The fox was in the shadows.

foxes, shadow

11. She had a red coat and bright eyes.
12. The fox was watching the hens.
13. Sturdy wire and strong boards would keep the chickens safe.
14. She needed to feed her pups.
15. She did not see the girl who was watching her.
16. That person wanted the animal to be her pet.
17. A horn on a car beeped loudly.
18. The small hunter picked up her ears.
19. An airplane roared overhead.
20. The little creature heard the noises.
21. She dashed off into the bushes.

PLURAL NOUNS ENDING IN *IES*

A. Proofread each sentence. Write the correct plural form of the nouns whose singular form ends in *y*.

Example:

Fernando and Haruo are buddy.

buddies

1. They have very different hobby.
2. Fernando collects penny, and Haruo trains puppy.
3. Fernando has lived in three city in Michigan.
4. Haruo has lived in three country in South America.
5. Fernando is friendly and dislikes bully.
6. Haruo likes to hear Fernando's many story.
7. Fernando loves birthday party.
8. Haruo watches plays and comedy on TV.
9. Fernando helps his mother bake many pastry.
10. Haruo helps his father make different jelly and jams.

PRACTICE

B. Revise the underlined nouns in each sentence. Write the singular form of any underlined plural noun. Write the plural form of any underlined singular noun.

Example:

Some <u>families</u> take vacations in the <u>country</u>.

family, countries

11. Dalton visits his grandmother in the <u>city</u> every summer.

12. Today the <u>sky</u> is clear and bright.

13. Dalton waters the <u>daisies</u> in the garden.

14. His grandmother cuts <u>lilies</u> for a bouquet.

15. Dalton meets old and new <u>buddies</u> at the park.

16. George invited Dalton to his birthday <u>party</u>.

17. Dalton has no <u>worries</u>.

18. He writes to his <u>family</u> every week.

19. There is a new <u>puppy</u> at his home.

20. His room has a fish tank full of <u>guppies</u>.

21. Dalton's grandmother works at the <u>library</u>.

22. Dalton likes to read <u>stories</u> about animals.

23. He also likes to read <u>mysteries</u>.

A. Read each sentence. Write the noun in parentheses ( ) that fits best.

Example:

Keisha has lost her two front (tooth, teeth).

   teeth

1. Keisha has gone to Dr. Chun since she was a small (child, children).

2. The (man, men) who lives next door goes to Dr. Chun, too.

3. Dr. Chun is a fine dentist and a friendly (woman, women).

4. She has toys including a mechanical (goose, geese) in her office.

5. Two of the toys are dancing (mouse, mice).

6. A big stuffed (ox, oxen) sits in a chair.

7. A cartoon about a little country (mouse, mice) hangs on the wall.

8. A pair of plastic (goose, geese) stand in the corner.

9. Many (child, children) like Dr. Chun.

10. She keeps her patients happy and their (tooth, teeth) healthy.

B. Look at the underlined noun in each sentence. Write the plural form of any underlined singular noun. Write the singular form of any underlined plural noun.

Examples:

Every child likes this kind of amusement park.

children

The mice there talk and sing.

mouse

11. A goose lays golden eggs near a tree with golden leaves.

12. A wolf brags about his sharp teeth.

13. A giant man waves.

14. His feet are as large as boats.

15. Beside him stands a friendly blue ox.

16. One woman lives in an old shoe.

17. Many children crowd around her.

18. An angry woman chases three mice.

A. Read the sentences. Write the possessive nouns.

Example:

Chester wanted to be the first to use the class's new computer.

class's

1. The room's new computer arrived today.
2. Elena plugged in the machine's keyboard.
3. The students' eyes opened wide.
4. The monitor's screen lit up.
5. It was the school's first color monitor!
6. Ms. Aboud asked for Chester's help.
7. Chester saw Joni's sad face.
8. He wondered what his friend's problem was.
9. "I don't understand the user's handbook," whispered Joni.
10. "Soon you'll be the class's computer expert!" said Chester.

B. Write each sentence. Underline the possessive noun.

Example:

Vivian's class visited the seashore.

Vivian's class visited the seashore.

11. That ocean's size surprised her.

12. The sun's light was bright.

13. Vivian took Juni's picture.

14. Then Juni took Vivian's picture.

15. The group's task was to observe tide pools.

16. "This one's waves are filling up this pool," Juni said.

17. The two girls' tide pool was busy.

18. A crab interrupted a water bug's stroll.

19. The bug ran away from the crab's snapping claws.

20. Vivian counted a starfish's legs.

21. Juni borrowed a friend's pencil.

22. She sketched a creature's shape.

23. Vivian wanted to touch a sea urchin's spines.

24. She remembered her teacher's instructions, though.

25. "Do not disturb this pool's residents!"

SINGULAR POSSESSIVE NOUNS

A. Write each possessive noun that is singular. Be careful. Not all of the sentences have a singular possessive noun.

Example:

Todd's friend Daniel was playing for the Bluebirds.

   Todd's

1. Daniel came up from the team's dugout.
2. He heard his teammates' cheers.
3. The pitcher tugged on his cap's bill.
4. Daniel remembered his coaches' instructions.
5. He swung at the pitcher's first pitch.
6. Daniel hit a ground ball to the shortstop's left.
7. The player's throw was too high.
8. It went over the first baseman's head.
9. Daniel's legs carried him safely to second base.
10. Later, Daniel scored the Bluebirds' first run.

B. Read these sentences. Revise the underlined words so that one of the words is a singular possessive noun.

Example:

The paws of Scooter were covered with pizza sauce.

Scooter's paws

11. The naughty dog had eaten the <u>dinner of the family</u>.
12. The <u>mother of Dina</u> was upset.
13. The <u>engine of her car</u> was not working.
14. The <u>store in town</u> had already closed.
15. Dina said she would solve that <u>problem of the day</u>.
16. She fastened the <u>strap of her helmet</u>.
17. She rode her bike to the <u>shop in the next town</u>.
18. The <u>stomach of her mother</u> was rumbling.
19. As she passed the <u>parking lot of her school</u>, she saw something in the road.
20. It was the <u>backpack of a student</u>.
21. Dina looked at the <u>cover of the backpack</u>.
22. The <u>name of the owner</u> was written on it.
23. Dina had found the <u>backpack of her best friend</u>!

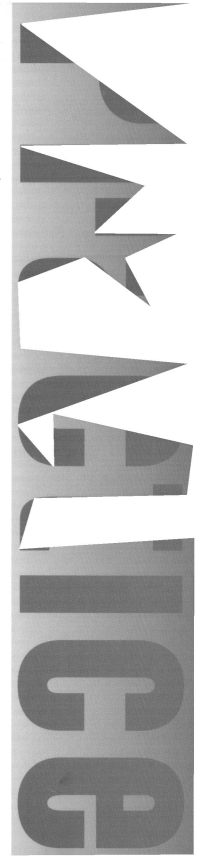

A. Read the sentences. Write the plural possessive nouns. Be careful. Not all sentences have a plural possessive noun.

Example:

Mr. Kozlov is the squirrels' best friend.

squirrels'

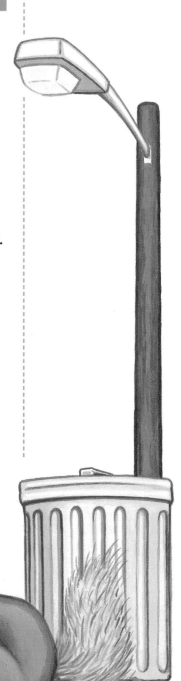

1. He sits beneath the trees' branches.
2. He pays no attention to the wind's cold, sharp air.
3. He watches the animals' quick movements.
4. Then he cracks the nuts' shells, one at a time.
5. He tosses the nuts near the oaks' roots.
6. He puts the empty shells into the park's trash can.
7. The nuts quickly disappear into the squirrels' mouths.
8. Finally, Mr. Kozlov's pockets are empty.
9. He leaves his friends' home.
10. The city's streetlights help him find his way.

B. Revise these sentences. Rewrite the underlined words so that one of the words is a plural possessive noun.

Example:

The smell of hamburgers made everyone hungry.

hamburgers' smell

11. Sami swept the sidewalks of his neighbors.
12. He heard the laughter of his sisters.
13. He saw the kites of two boys.
14. Mrs. Gomez lit the barbecues of the cooks.
15. She made the crispy shells of the tacos.
16. The residents of the apartments came to the party.
17. The pets of the parents were not invited.
18. The behavior of the pets had not been good last year.
19. The cones of the workers blocked off the street.
20. The engines of the cars were all silent.
21. The radios of the teenagers were all tuned to the same station.
22. The feet of the dancers moved quickly.
23. The dance by the twins was a big hit.
24. The party of the families was a big success!

A. Write the pronouns in these sentences.

Example:

Edwin called me Friday morning.

me

1. "We want you to come with us to the lake!" he exclaimed.

2. "Do you have room for me in the car?" I asked.

3. "Yes, we are borrowing Aunt Lydia's van," he answered.

4. "Are you bringing a fishing pole?" I asked.

5. "Yes, Mom and I are going to rent a rowboat for fishing," Edwin replied.

6. Then he said, "When we went to the lake in May, she caught a huge bass."

7. "Would you ask her to give me a fishing lesson?" I asked.

8. "She will be glad to teach you," Edwin said.

9. "I would love to go with you tomorrow," I said finally.

10. "Great!" said Edwin. "We will pick you up at 4 A.M."

B. Read each pair of sentences. Write a pronoun that makes sense in the blank.

Example:

This bridge is being painted. _____ must not get rusty.

　It

11. Susan is a painter. _____ paints bridges.
12. The paint keeps the bridge looking clean. _____ also keeps rust from forming.
13. Brett checks the bridge. _____ looks for trouble spots.
14. Rust forms all the time. _____ forms where water settles on steel.
15. Susan climbs a ladder. _____ climbs slowly.
16. She paints an old bolt. _____ is very rusty.
17. Brett looks at the bridge cables. _____ help support the bridge.
18. You and I watch the workers. _____ think they are brave.
19. Drivers see the work truck. _____ slow down.
20. Now Susan and Brett are painting a bridge tower. _____ is many feet high!
21. Susan and Brett are high above the river. _____ are not afraid.

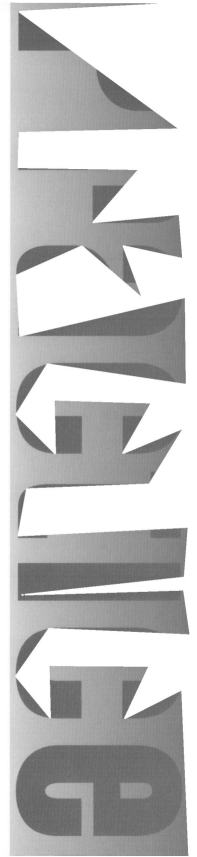

A. Read the sentences. Write the singular pronouns.

Example:

I went with Natalie and Matt to the school carnival.

   I

1. Natalie and I were at a picnic table.
2. She was telling me a joke.
3. Suddenly I heard a whistle blow.
4. "The three-legged race is starting!" Natalie yelled to me.
5. She and I ran to the playing field at top speed.
6. Matt waved wildly to me.
7. "Will you hop with me?" he asked.
8. Natalie looked at me, and I looked at her.
9. "I am Natalie's partner," I told him.
10. Matt raced with Robert, but Natalie and I won by a foot.

B. Read each pair of sentences. Write the singular pronoun that fits with the meaning of the second sentence.

Example:

The subway train rumbled toward the station. _____ stopped at the platform.

   It

11. Ned was going to a soccer match. _____ wore a jacket.

12. Ned had been waiting for twenty minutes. _____ had written a letter to pass the time.

13. Ned's mom had been reading. She had brought a newspaper with _____.

14. Ned got on the train. Ned's mom followed _____.

15. Ned stood in the crowded train car. _____ held on to a pole.

16. Ned's mom studied a map. _____ told Ned they would get off at the next stop.

17. A moment later the train slowed down. _____ was not at any station.

18. Then the train began moving faster. _____ pulled into the station.

19. Ned wanted to run ahead. _____ stayed close to his mom, though.

20. Ned spotted his mom from the field. _____ had a front row seat.

A. Write the plural pronouns in these sentences.

Example:

"I am glad the teacher put us in charge of art supplies," Shirley said to Omar.

us

1. "We will go to the pond today and paint," Shirley said.
2. "Won't the other class join us?" asked Omar.
3. "No, they will paint at the park today," Shirley said.
4. "Should we count the easels?" Omar asked.
5. "No, I am sure they are all here," Shirley answered.
6. "I am going to count them, anyway," said Omar.
7. The two of them walked to the supply closet.
8. They found that two easels were borrowed by the other class.
9. "We were smart to check," said Shirley.
10. "Those missing easels could have caused problems for us," she told Omar.

B. Read each pair of sentences. Write a plural pronoun that would make sense in each blank.

Example:

Lorena pointed at the clouds. "_____ look dangerous!" she said.

   They

11. "It looks like rain. _____ should all run to the bus," Lorena said.

12. Kim said, "Our teachers asked us to find all the plants on the list. _____ will be unhappy if we don't."

13. "Storms can be dangerous," Lorena said. "I want _____ to be safe."

14. Heavy rain began to fall on the girls. _____ ran toward the bus.

15. "I see blackberry bushes and a sugar pine tree!" said Kim. "_____ are both on our list!"

16. "This is no time to stop!" said Lorena. "_____ will get very wet."

17. The girls reached the school bus. "_____ were worried about you!" their teachers said.

18. Kim told the teachers she had not found all the plants on the list. _____ told her not to worry.

19. Lorena pointed to the trees outside. "_____ have needed rain for some time," she said.

20. "Everyone is here," said the bus driver. "_____ can leave now."

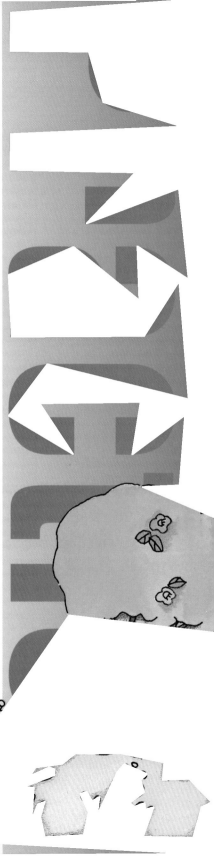

SUBJECT PRONOUNS

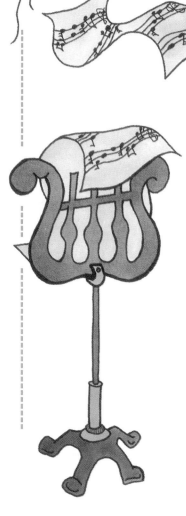

A. Write the subject pronouns in these sentences.

Example:

I rehearsed outside with Jan last Wednesday.

   I

1. We practiced all ten of our concert pieces.
2. She set down her bow and went to get some water.
3. I saw a parrot fly into the bandstand.
4. It picked up Jan's sheet music and began to fly away.
5. I yelled, "Hey, bird, put Jan's music down!"
6. I think my yelling surprised the parrot.
7. It dropped the paper.
8. We put Jan's music back on her stand.
9. She laughed at the story of the music-loving parrot.
10. Will we see the parrot on the day of our concert?

B. Revise each sentence. Replace the underlined word or words with a subject pronoun.

Example:

<u>Anton</u> puts on his air tank.

He puts on his air tank.

11. <u>The Red Sea</u> is warm and salty.
12. <u>Many unusual fish</u> live there.
13. <u>Anton</u> will take pictures under the water.
14. <u>His sister Pam</u> will develop them.
15. <u>Anton and Pam</u> spot a coral reef beneath the water.
16. <u>The reef</u> has brightly colored fish around it.
17. <u>The skillful diver</u> slips into the water.
18. <u>A jellyfish</u> is there.
19. <u>Anton's sister</u> shouts a warning.
20. <u>Anton</u> swims out of the way.
21. <u>The diver</u> breathes a sigh of relief.
22. <u>Soldierfish</u> swim by.
23. <u>Anton</u> photographs the rose-colored fish.
24. <u>Anton's talent</u> is well known.
25. Tomorrow <u>Pam and Anton</u> will photograph fish together.

A. Write the object pronouns in these sentences.

Example:

Carola's father took her to the amusement park.

her

1. Carola led him over to the speedway.
2. "This is the ride for me!" Carola said.
3. Carola's father bought two tickets for them.
4. She gave them to the ride operator.
5. "Put us in the fastest car, please," Carola said to the operator.
6. "Give us the slowest car," Carola's father said.
7. The operator smiled at them.
8. "Promise me you will not break the sound barrier," said the operator to Carola.
9. He put them into a fast red sports car.
10. Carola's father drove it around the track swiftly but safely.

B. Revise each sentence. Replace the underlined word or words with an object pronoun.

Example:

Cathy and I saw <u>the tortoises</u> first.

  them

11. I have been to <u>this beach</u> before.

12. I have never seen <u>a tortoise</u> here.

13. They live with <u>other tortoises</u>.

14. Many tortoises share <u>one area</u>.

15. They dig <u>tunnels</u>.

16. Look for <u>a pile of dirt</u> at the tunnel's mouth.

17. A tortoise dug <u>another tunnel</u> with its feet.

18. Cathy went to tell <u>Ranger Leo</u> the news.

19. Ranger Leo came back with <u>Cathy</u>.

20. We counted <u>tortoises</u> for six hours.

21. We carefully arranged <u>our cameras</u>.

22. I asked permission from <u>Ranger Leo</u> first.

23. He gave permission to <u>this photographer</u>.

24. We will develop <u>the photos</u> tomorrow morning.

25. Then we will write to environmental groups about <u>this tortoise</u>.

ADJECTIVES

A. Write the adjective or adjectives in each sentence. Do not include *a*, *an*, or *the*.

Example:

A long time ago, people believed the earth was flat.

long, flat

1. Magellan was a brave captain.
2. He commanded a fleet of five ships.
3. There were difficult problems.
4. Many crewmen would not follow orders.
5. A fierce storm destroyed one ship.
6. There wasn't enough food.
7. The unhappy crew stopped for food and water in the Philippines.
8. The sailors were hungry and thirsty.
9. One ship returned home to Spain.
10. The journey proved that the earth is round.

B. Write the adjective in each sentence. Do not include *a*, *an*, or *the*. Also write the noun the adjective describes.

Example:

A lively goat jumped from rock to rock.

lively, goat

11. The goat made four jumps in a row.
12. Lucy took pictures of the graceful animal.
13. The goat went behind a huge boulder.
14. Lucy put a new roll of film into the camera.
15. She watched for sudden movements on the mountainside.
16. Three goats appeared on the trail.
17. Lucy admired their white coats.
18. She focused her small camera.
19. She took five pictures quickly.
20. The suspicious goats hopped away from Lucy.
21. They made long shadows on the rocks.
22. The red sun set behind the mountains.
23. Lucy buttoned her heavy coat.
24. She happily began the long hike down the trail.
25. She knew she had taken wonderful pictures.

ADJECTIVES THAT TELL *HOW MANY*

A. Write each adjective that tells how many. Some adjectives are made up of two words.

Example:

The distance from Earth to Mars is about fifty million miles.

fifty million

1. Several astronauts climb aboard the spacecraft.
2. One billion people watch the launch on TV.
3. Everyone counts out loud during the final ten seconds.
4. Three powerful rockets blast the crew into space.
5. The journey to Mars takes many months.
6. The crew members eat at least two meals a day.
7. They sleep for seven hours every night.
8. Finally, five astronauts land on Mars.
9. The temperature is one hundred degrees below zero!

B. Revise these sentences. Replace each blank with an adjective that tells how many.

Example:

I will become a famous explorer when I am _____ years old.

fourteen

10. I will have _____ partners.

11. We will travel _____ miles.

12. Our journey will last _____ days.

13. We will pack _____ pounds of food.

14. I shall bring _____ pairs of shoes.

15. On the hottest day, the temperature will be _____ degrees.

16. On the coldest day, the temperature will be _____ degrees below zero.

17. We will check our map _____ times.

18. We will cook _____ meals.

19. We will use _____ feet of rope.

20. We will discover _____ kinds of plants.

21. We will take photographs of _____ rare animals.

22. We will find a treasure worth _____ dollars.

23. Our pictures will be on the covers of _____ magazines.

PRACTICE

ADJECTIVES THAT TELL *WHAT KIND*

A. List each adjective that tells what kind.

Example:

I wrote a long letter to my sister.

long

1. It tells about an interesting experience I am having.
2. I'm learning new things every day in camp.
3. The unit is called the Green Giants.
4. We painted a large sign with the name.
5. You would have a great time here.
6. We helped build a wooden path for the trail.
7. The unit found a hidden nest.
8. Tiny rabbits were in it.
9. We were a silent group of observers.
10. Look in the envelope for a funny souvenir.

B. Write the adjective in each sentence that tells what kind. Also, write the noun that it describes.

Example:

Light rain falls on the plains.

light, rain

11. The tall grasses bend in the wind.
12. The rain moistens the dry earth.
13. Umaru drives his truck along a narrow road.
14. He is headed for market in the busy city.
15. The truck is loaded with heavy sacks of soybeans.
16. A large piece of canvas keeps them dry.
17. Umaru cannot sell wet soybeans.
18. He worries about the dark clouds.
19. Suddenly a sharp stone punctures a tire!
20. He must change the flat tire.
21. Umaru tries to turn the rusty bolts.
22. It is hard to remove the damaged tire.
23. Then he remembers the red can he bought at the store.
24. Umaru sprays its special mixture into the tire.
25. Umaru's difficult problem is solved!

A. Write the articles in these sentences.

Example:

A huge bass leaps out of the water.

  A, the

1. Chesapeake Bay is home to a great many creatures.
2. In the 1960s, the bay was becoming polluted.
3. Chesapeake Bay is now a cleaner and safer place for wild creatures.
4. An otter runs along the shore.
5. An eagle glides across the sky.
6. An old turtle dives off a log.
7. A beautiful swan spreads its wings.
8. Oysters live on the rocky floor of the bay.
9. An osprey dives into the water.
10. A fish is the osprey's target.

B. Write an article that would fit well in the sentence.

Example:

Loggerhead turtles are _____ endangered species.

an

11. _____ female turtle laid her eggs last night.

12. First, she dug _____ hole in _____ sand.

13. Then, she laid her eggs in _____ hole.

14. She covered _____ eggs with sand.

15. _____ female turtle does not stay at the nest.

16. It is against _____ law to disturb these nests.

17. However, Alfredo is _____ wildlife professional.

18. He alone may take _____ eggs.

19. Alfredo digs in _____ sand and finds _____ nest!

20. He puts _____ eggs into _____ ice chest.

21. Then he fills _____ chest with wet sand.

22. Alfredo will keep _____ ice chest in _____ cool place until _____ eggs hatch.

23. He will then release _____ baby turtles into _____ ocean.

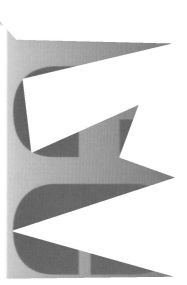

ADJECTIVES THAT COMPARE: -ER, -EST

A. Read the sentences. Write each adjective that compares two things.

Example:

This crocodile is longer than that one.

longer

1. Alligators have rounder snouts than crocodiles.
2. Crocodile eggs are bigger than hens' eggs.
3. The crocodile is one of the largest of all reptiles.
4. It is faster than an alligator.
5. Crocodiles can stay under water the longest.

B. Write each adjective that compares more than two things. There are four.

Example:

The goby is one of the smallest of all fish.

smallest

6. The giraffe is the tallest mammal of all.
7. The African elephant is larger than the Asian elephant.
8. The cheetah is the fastest land animal.
9. Dogs are the easiest mammals to train.
10. Bears are the strongest mammals.

C. Revise each sentence. Change the word in parentheses ( ) to its correct form.

Example:

Otters are the (cute) animals of all in the zoo.

cutest

11. This otter is (fast) than the other one.
12. A mongoose's strike is (quick) than a snake's.
13. Are owls the (wise) of all birds?
14. That tortoise is (old) than any other animal here.
15. Its shell is (thick) than a turtle's.
16. Which of all the snakes is the (long)?
17. The new snake house is (large) than the old one.
18. Which bear has the (thick) fur of all the bears?
19. Penguins live in the (cold) of all places on earth.
20. House cats have the (soft) fur of all.
21. Are chicken eggs (small) than ostrich eggs?
22. Is the shrew the (small) mammal in all the world?

A. Read the sentences. Write only the adjectives that compare two things.

Example:

Tropical fish are more colorful than Arctic fish.

more colorful

1. Salmon are more rapid swimmers than perch.
2. Great white sharks are more dangerous to swimmers than nurse sharks.
3. Guppies are the most popular fish.
4. Catfish are more common than sharks.
5. The grass carp is more useful than many other fish because it eats weeds.

B. Write only the adjectives that compare more than two things.

6. Rays have the most unusual shape of any fish.
7. The electric eel produces the most powerful electric charge of any creature.
8. An eel is more difficult to hold than a trout.
9. Tuna may be the most common fish we eat.
10. Is fish the most healthy meat there is?

C. Complete each sentence. Write *more* or *most* to make a correct comparison.

Example:

Amphibians may be the _____ interesting creatures in the world.

   most

11. The salamander is the _____ unusual amphibian. It breathes through its skin.

12. Are frogs _____ unusual than salamanders?

13. Do frogs have the _____ accurate tongues for catching insects?

14. A chameleon's tongue is _____ accurate than a frog's.

15. The frogs that glide through the air are the _____ amazing of all.

16. Frogs can be _____ colorful than many other creatures.

17. One small red frog is the _____ poisonous creature on earth.

18. Chameleons are _____ amazing than frogs because they can change color.

19. Frogs have _____ beautiful voices than any other animal.

20. Some think a frog's voice is _____ bothersome than any other animal's voice.

21. Frogs are the _____ helpful amphibians you can have in your garden.

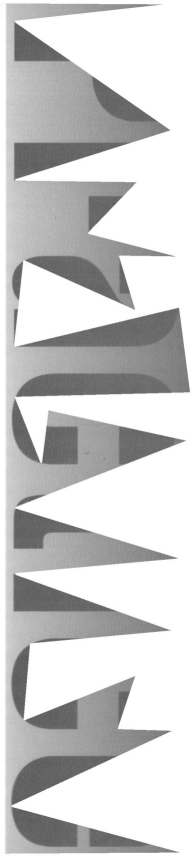

PRACTICE

VERBS

A. Read the sentences. Write the verb in each one.

Example:

Mrs. Stein makes costumes for actors in plays.

  makes

1. Before the school play, Mrs. Stein visits our class.
2. Each child drew a picture of a costume.
3. Last year, Ling painted a picture of a bumblebee.
4. The bumblebee looked very busy!
5. Mrs. Stein unrolled some yellow felt.
6. She and Ling cut two ovals from the cloth.
7. Mrs. Stein sewed the ovals together.
8. Ling attached black paper for stripes.
9. Two pieces of plastic formed the wings.
10. Ling buzzed through the room in her bee costume.

B. Read each pair of sentences. In the blank, write a verb that would make sense.

Example:

Frogs are amphibians. They _____ both on land and in water.

   live

11. Elkin's yard has a garden and a creek. He _____ outside all day.

12. The garden needs water to grow. Elkin _____ the garden.

13. Elkin's grandfather planted flowers there. They _____ quickly.

14. Frogs in the creek croak loudly. Elkin _____ them in the evening.

15. Tadpoles are young frogs. They _____ in the water, just like fish.

16. One day Elkin found a rabbit's nest. The mother _____ in front of him.

17. Elkin wondered how many baby rabbits were in the nest. He _____ eight of them.

18. Elkin knew the mother would come right back. He _____ away from the nest.

ACTION VERBS

A. Read each sentence. Write the action verb.

Example:

Travelers in Africa often see ostriches.

see

1. Ostriches run very fast.
2. They jump high, too.
3. They kick with their strong legs.
4. Lions chase ostriches.
5. The ostriches usually escape.
6. These tall birds build nests on the sand.
7. First, the male ostrich digs a hole.
8. Then a female lays several large eggs.
9. The male warms the eggs with his body.
10. The chicks hatch after about forty-five days.

B. Revise each sentence. In the blank, write an action verb that makes sense.

Example:

Anteaters _____ ants with their sticky tongues.
   catch

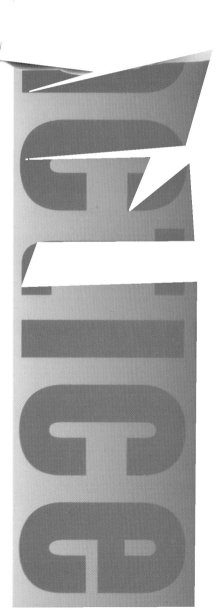

11. Beavers _____ dams in streams.

12. Bats _____ at night.

13. Frogs _____ loudly.

14. Roosters _____ noisily in the morning.

15. Monkeys _____ from branch to branch in the tall trees.

16. Cheetahs _____ very fast.

17. Kangaroos _____ high and far.

18. Some whales _____ thousands of miles across the ocean.

19. Woodpeckers _____ holes in trees.

20. Squirrels _____ nuts in the ground.

21. Pandas _____ bamboo and many other plants.

22. Owls _____ after mice.

23. Skunks _____ a bad smell when they are attacked.

24. Lizards _____ quietly on rocks in the sun.

A. Write the main verb in each sentence.

Example:

Caleb and Maya have packed their equipment.

packed

1. Maya has planned this day for months.
2. She and Caleb have traveled to the sea.
3. Caleb had collected more than two hundred different shells.
4. He has placed them all in boxes.
5. He has searched the whole reef.
6. They have used special equipment for this search.
7. Maya has stored her shells in a sack.
8. She has picked the best ones.
9. Maya has adjusted her snorkel.
10. She had cleaned it carefully.

B. Write the verbs in each sentence. Underline the main verb.

Example:

David has arrived at Uncle Gary's ranch.

   has <u>arrived</u>

11. David had visited him there three times before.
12. He had arrived by jet.
13. They have unpacked David's things.
14. Uncle Gary has raised llamas on his ranch for eight years.
15. They have helped him in many ways.
16. Uncle Gary has traded their wool for equipment.
17. The llamas have provided transportation, too.
18. David has gone on a camping trip.
19. The llamas have walked this way before.
20. They have enjoyed the hike.
21. David and Uncle Gary have cooked a meal.
22. They have finished eating now.

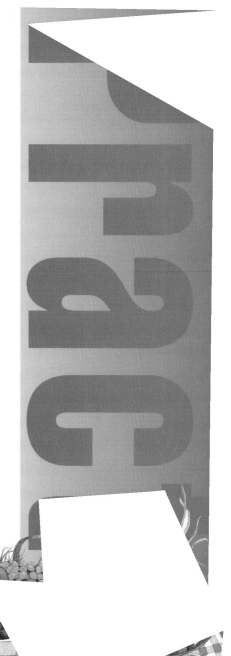

HELPING VERBS

A. Write the helping verb in each sentence.

Example:

We have watched a sunrise today.

have

1. I have enjoyed the bright colors of dawn.
2. My sister Ann has joined me.
3. She had baked muffins for breakfast.
4. We have hiked to the top of a mountain.
5. Pink streaks of light have filled the sky.
6. Geese had honked at each other for hours earlier.
7. Ann and I have worked together outside before.
8. We have looked at the whole countryside.
9. Ann has finished her painting of the geese.
10. I have framed mine.

B. Write the verbs in each sentence. Underline the helping verb.

Example:

The ape has moved swiftly through the treetops.

has moved

11. These apes have lived in tropical forests for thousands of years.
12. My camera has recorded their graceful motions.
13. One of them had slipped.
14. Has it injured its leg?
15. No, it has climbed back up the tree.
16. Another ape had helped it.
17. One ape has provided food for its neighbor.
18. They have liked their view from the treetops.
19. I have used all my film.
20. We had learned much from this project.

PRESENT - TIME VERBS

A. Read each sentence. Write the present-time form of the verb shown in parentheses ( ).

Example:

My cat (arched/arches) his back.

arches

1. I (look/looked) at him.
2. He (sees/saw) something.
3. I (thought/think) it is a rope.
4. The rope (surprised/surprises) me.
5. It (moves/moved) by itself.
6. I (call/called) my mom.
7. She (knew/knows) about snakes.
8. This breed (hunted/hunts) only mice.
9. Mom (wraps/wrapped) it in a towel.
10. She (put/puts) it back outside.

B. Revise each sentence. Change the underlined verb so it tells about the present.

Example:

The chickens <u>walked</u> out of the henhouse.

The chickens walk out of the henhouse.

11. The chickens <u>clucked</u> a hello.
12. They <u>stretched</u> their wings.
13. Two hens <u>pecked</u> at some grain.
14. A chicken with white feathers <u>gobbled</u> up a slug.
15. The puppy <u>jumped</u> up and down.
16. He <u>barked</u> loudly at the chickens.
17. The chickens <u>scattered</u> in the yard.
18. The farm owner <u>greeted</u> the chickens with a cheerful wave.
19. She <u>tossed</u> them some broccoli and squash.
20. They <u>nibbled</u> the vegetables happily.
21. A large hen <u>scratched</u> at the dirt in the yard.
22. A chick <u>followed</u> her.
23. Two other chickens <u>wandered</u> over.
24. A little hen <u>discovered</u> a group of tasty bugs.
25. She <u>shared</u> the bugs with all the other hens.

A. Read the sentences. Write each past-time verb.

Example:

Shana created a number trick for her math project.

created

1. First, she sketched a triangle on a sheet of paper.
2. Then she traced a circle at each corner of the triangle.
3. Next, she added a circle in the middle of each side.
4. Shana jotted a number from 1 to 6 inside each circle.
5. The three numbers on each side of the triangle totaled 12.
6. Tim checked Shana's addition carefully.
7. Shana demonstrated her number trick to the class.
8. Some students solved the puzzle quickly.
9. Shana's teacher praised her project.
10. Later, some other students invented their own number tricks.

B. Revise each sentence. Change the verb in parentheses ( ) to its past-time form.

Example:

Rita (construct) a puzzle yesterday.
constructed

11. First, she (sketch) a triangle on a piece of paper.
12. Next, she (mark) five steps on each side.
13. Then she (show) a step at the top.
14. She (reproduce) the drawing onto a block of wood.
15. Her father quickly (saw) the wood.
16. Rita (move) the finished puzzle.
17. She (place) a red marker on each step on the right side.
18. She (arrange) a blue marker on each step on the left side.
19. Rita (complete) the puzzle on her first try!
20. Then she (hand) the puzzle to her father.
21. After an hour, Rita's dad (ask) for her help.

A. Read each sentence. Choose the correct form of the verb in parentheses ( ).

Example:

We (drove/driven) to a museum by the sea.

drove

1. It (gave/given) me a new idea for a hobby.
2. Mom (drove/driven) me to the supermarket.
3. "We have (eaten/ate) dinner already," she said.
4. We (went/goes) anyway.
5. I had (gone/went) into the store.
6. I (came/comes) out with an empty milk jug.
7. We (drove/drives) home.
8. I have (gave/given) the model I made to my mom.
9. "How (done/did) you get a model ship inside this small jug?" she asked.
10. "I have (do/done) the impossible," I grinned.

B. Revise these sentences. Change the underlined present-time verbs to the correct form of the past-time verb.

Example:

I <u>do</u> research for my report yesterday.
   did

11. I have <u>eat</u> many foods.
12. I thought I had <u>do</u> all my research.
13. Our dog Rusty <u>come</u> into the kitchen.
14. I <u>give</u> him a delicious dog biscuit.
15. "Rusty, what <u>do</u> you think of it?" I asked.
16. He <u>go</u> to the food cabinet.
17. "I have just <u>give</u> you the last one," I said.
18. I had <u>go</u> into the garage to speak to my dad.
19. A minute later, Dad <u>drive</u> me to the store.
20. When I had <u>comes</u> out, I had a present for Rusty.
21. He <u>eat</u> and <u>eat</u> those special treats.

233

MORE IRREGULAR VERBS

A. Read each sentence. Change the verb in parentheses ( ) to its correct form.

Example:

I once (see) tall statues in a place called Easter Island.

saw

1. Last year a plane (take) us to visit this faraway place.
2. Our tour guide has (say) these statues are a mystery.
3. Scientists had (think) they were carved by local island people.
4. Yesterday the tour bus (ride) from place to place.
5. A few times we got off the bus and (run) around.
6. I (see) statues everywhere I looked.
7. Each one's face (have) a serious look.
8. I have (take) many photographs.
9. Back then, I had (think) they would make nice postcards.
10. I have not (have) them developed yet.

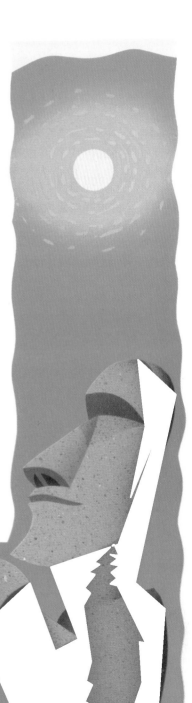

B. Read each sentence. Choose the verb in parentheses ( ) that is correct.

Example:

Lyle (taken/took) a trip to Philadelphia last weekend.

   took

11. He (ride/rode) in the front seat next to his dad.

12. He had (have/had) his pet parrot in the back seat.

13. Every time the parrot had (saw/seen) something it liked, it squawked.

14. Lyle and his dad (thought/thinks) for a while.

15. Then Lyle's dad (have/had) a good idea.

16. "Teach it to say hello," he (say/said).

17. As they (ridden/rode) along, Lyle taught the parrot the word *hello*.

18. It (took/taken) a few hours.

19. Lyle had almost (run/ran) out of hope.

20. Suddenly, the parrot (seen/saw) another bird.

21. "Hello! Hello!" it (say/said).

22. Lyle was glad he had (taken/took) his father's advice.

A. Write the form of the verb *be* in each sentence.

Example:

Yesterday the bus was on time.

was

1. Today the bus is late.
2. The streets were noisy by 8 o'clock yesterday morning.
3. From my window I see the streets are quiet.
4. I am already late for school.
5. My friends are probably all there by now.
6. The bus driver is usually nice.
7. Why is everything so odd today?
8. Yesterday was Friday, not Thursday!
9. Today is not a school day!
10. The bus and I are not late.

B. Read each sentence. Write a form of the verb *be* that correctly completes each sentence.

Example:

Today my boots and mittens _____ in the closet.

   are

11. Today _____ December 20.
12. Today's weather _____ warm.
13. There _____ many hours of daylight left.
14. Some people _____ at the beach.
15. We _____ at a picnic all day yesterday.
16. December _____ usually a cold month.
17. Last December, snow _____ on the ground.
18. The sky _____ gray this time last year.
19. Today the sky _____ blue.
20. Last December the only kangaroos near us _____ in a warm room at the zoo.
21. Today some kangaroos _____ in the field across from our home.
22. Why _____ December so different this year?
23. This year we _____ in the Southern Hemisphere.
24. Summertime _____ in December here.
25. We _____ in Australia!

ADVERBS

A. Write the adverb in each sentence.

Example:

Teresa often visits her grandmother in Hawaii.

often

1. Teresa arrived at the Hilo Airport yesterday.
2. Grandma NeNe greeted Teresa warmly.
3. Now the two of them are making flower necklaces.
4. Teresa runs ahead to gather pink lokelani flowers.
5. Grandma NeNe swiftly threads a curved needle with string.
6. Teresa has already lined up the flowers.
7. Teresa carefully pokes the needle through each flower.
8. Grandma NeNe expertly knots the ends of the string.
9. Teresa proudly wears the beautiful necklace.
10. Grandma NeNe stands nearby.

B. Revise each sentence. Replace the underlined adverb with another adverb of your choice.

Example:

Marco's mother <u>usually</u> practices the piano.

Marco's mother <u>often</u> practices the piano.

11. Marco <u>eagerly</u> helps his mother.
12. He <u>carefully</u> turns the pages of her music book.
13. Marco's mother plays <u>skillfully</u>.
14. <u>Sometimes</u> she stops, though.
15. Marco <u>immediately</u> checks the music book.
16. He finds the next notes <u>quickly</u>.
17. <u>Then</u> he locates the correct piano keys.
18. He <u>lightly</u> touches each key.
19. Marco and his mother <u>always</u> laugh at mistakes.
20. They sing the words of a song <u>cheerfully</u>.
21. Marco looks <u>outside</u> and smiles.
22. A crowd has gathered <u>nearby</u>.

A. Read each sentence. Write *to, too,* or *two.*

Example:

Last winter Uma and her mother went _____ Norway.

  to

1. They visited their _____ friends, Marta and Bjorn.

2. They flew _____ a village north of the Arctic Circle.

3. They arrived in a village at _____ o'clock in the afternoon.

4. The stars were out, and the moon was rising, _____.

5. Marta said the sun would not rise again for _____ more weeks.

6. Bjorn and Marta invited their guests _____ a masked ball.

7. On the day of the first sunrise, Bjorn gave a party mask _____ Uma.

8. Marta gave her a mask, _____.

9. Uma showed one of her masks _____ her mother.

10. The four friends hurried _____ the center of town.

B. Proofread each sentence, and rewrite it correctly.

Example:

I will give a journal too Lisa for her birthday.

I will give a journal to Lisa for her birthday.

11. I will give her a nice pen, two.
12. Those too things will be a good present.
13. Lisa gave a journal too me last year.
14. I write a page or to in it every day.
15. I took it two my aunt's home this summer.
16. She keeps a journal, to.
17. She read parts of her old journal too me.
18. One part told about her trip two Jamaica.
19. She stayed for to months.
20. My aunt is a good writer and a good cook, two.
21. She gave one of her favorite recipes too me.
22. I cooked it and ate it, to.
23. The too of us enjoyed being together.
24. Soon I will go too Lisa's party.
25. I will walk the to blocks two her house.

YOUR, YOU'RE

A. Read the sentences. Write *your* or *you're* to complete each sentence.

Example:

Wouldn't it be great if you and _____ friends could make all the rules for a day?

your

1. If _____ in the country of Turkey on April 23, you will enjoy Children's Day there.

2. You and _____ classmates might be elected to run the government.

3. All the laws would be _____ responsibility for one day.

4. Would you ask _____ classmates to vote for you on Children's Day?

5. On Children's Day _____ transportation is free.

6. On that day _____ also allowed into the movies for free.

7. _____ stomach might ache from eating too much free ice cream.

8. If _____ visiting from another country, you can take part in a parade.

9. Perhaps _____ family will have a chance to visit Turkey someday.

10. _____ likely to remember _____ visit to Turkey.

B. Read each sentence. Write the word in parentheses ( ) that completes each sentence correctly.

Example:

"(Your/You're) up next, Wei," the coach said.
  You're

11. "Here's (your/you're) favorite bat," said Roger.

12. "I know (your/you're) going to get a hit," he said.

13. "Keep (your/you're) eye on the ball," the coach yelled.

14. "(Your/You're) going to get a hit," Wei told himself.

15. "I can hit (your/you're) fastball," Wei thought.

16. "(Your/You're) not going to get me out!" Wei said silently.

17. "I knew I could hit (your/you're) fastball!" Wei said as he smacked the ball hard.

18. "(Your/You're) the champ," the catcher said to Wei as he scored the winning run.

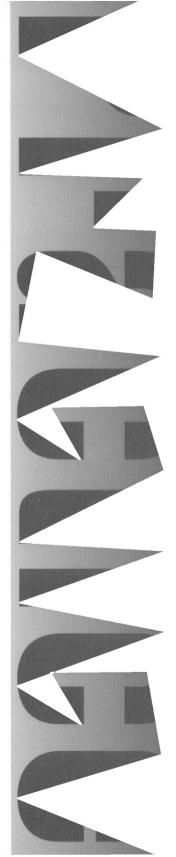

A. Read each sentence. Decide whether *its* or *it's* would be correct in the blank.

Example:

_____ really raining hard!

  It's

1. _____ a good thing I remembered my umbrella today!

2. I will take my umbrella out of _____ case.

3. The case won't open because _____ snap is stuck.

4. _____ hard to open a snap when your hands are wet.

5. Now _____ time for me to open my umbrella!

6. _____ going to feel good to be protected from the rain!

7. I'm trying to open my umbrella, but _____ not working.

8. _____ pole is bent.

9. There! I've fixed my umbrella, and _____ open at last!

10. Now _____ not raining anymore.

B. Proofread each sentence, and write it correctly. Correct the spelling or capitalization of each underlined word. Some sentences are correct.

Example:

its my turn to use the computer!

It's my turn to use the computer!

11. A computer stores information in it's memory.

12. its important to know how much memory your computer has.

13. This computer game is good because it's an educational game.

14. You cannot play this game on your computer because it's memory is too small.

15. it's time to add some memory to your computer!

16. Mom says it's easy to add memory to a computer.

17. If you put this chip into your computer, you will increase the size of it's memory.

18. Let's test your computer to see if Its new memory chip is working.

19. Great! Its working perfectly!

20. I like this game because it's pictures are colorful!

21. Now its time to stop playing the game.

22. Please put the game disk back in it's box.

23. Your computer has a screen saver on Its main menu.

THEIR, THERE, THEY'RE

A. Read each sentence. Decide whether *their*, *there*, or *they're* is correct, and write the missing word.

Example:

Our grandparents want us to know more about _____ lives.

their

1. _____ writing a book for us.
2. The book is a history of _____ lives.
3. They keep the book at _____ house.
4. We go over _____ for dinner on Sundays.
5. Grandma and Grandpa have put _____ old photographs in the book.
6. _____ very interesting to look at.
7. _____ is my favorite picture of Grandma.
8. I wish I had been with them _____ at the Seattle World's Fair.
9. _____ both great storytellers.
10. Sometimes they share _____ memories with us before they write them.

B. Proofread each sentence, and write it correctly. Correct the spelling of each underlined word.

Example:

Elephants are famous for <u>there</u> good memory.

Elephants are famous for their good memory.

11. Elephants from Asia are very useful because of <u>there</u> strength and intelligence.

12. <u>Theyre</u> used as work animals in Thailand.

13. They haul logs through the forest <u>their</u>.

14. It's not easy to prove how good <u>there</u> memory really is.

15. <u>their</u> able to remember many commands.

16. Dogs use <u>they're</u> memory, too.

17. They remember the scent of <u>there</u> owners.

18. <u>Their</u> able to remember where home is, too.

19. Some dogs find <u>there</u> way back home from hundreds of miles away.

20. No one is sure how <u>their</u> able to do this.

21. Dolphins have large brains for <u>they're</u> body size.

22. <u>Their</u> very intelligent animals.

23. <u>They're</u> language is made up of clicks, squeaks, and whistles.

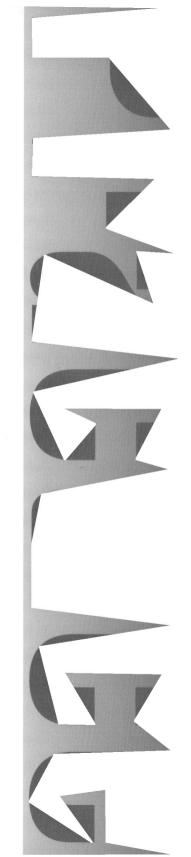

COMMA AFTER INTRODUCTORY WORDS

A. Write each sentence. Add a comma after the introductory word.

Example:

"Well it's time to open the photo album," said Ben.

"Well, it's time to open the photo album," said Ben.

1. "Yes I have been looking forward to this," said Joni.

2. "Well do you recognize that person?" said Ben.

3. "No I don't," Noli replied.

4. "Yes that is my cousin Jonny," Max replied.

5. "Well have you ever met him, Joni?"

6. "Well I must have met him, but I don't remember him," she replied as she looked at photos.

7. "Yes let's look at the photos of our trip to New York," Ben said.

8. "No I would rather see the photos of our visit to the Grand Canyon," Max said.

B. Read each sentence. Write an introductory word that would make sense in the blank. Remember to add a comma.

Example:

"_____ I remember our visit to Finland," said Ruth. "Do you remember it, Bela?"

Yes,

9. "_____ I do," said Bela. "We went with Grandma in 1992."

10. "_____ we went in 1993," said Ruth. "We left on Valentine's Day."

11. "_____ we left on St. Patrick's Day," said Bela. "That's why you wore a green dress!"

12. "_____ I think you're wrong," Ruth replied. "I'm sure I wore a red dress because it was Valentine's Day!"

13. "_____ here is a picture of us getting on the plane in Ohio," said Bela.

14. "_____ this is a picture of us getting on the plane in Helsinki," said Ruth.

15. "_____ you're wrong, Ruth," said Bela. "It must be Cleveland because you're wearing a green dress!"

16. "_____ you wouldn't remember that," said Bela.

17. "_____ I would," said Ruth. "I have a very good memory."

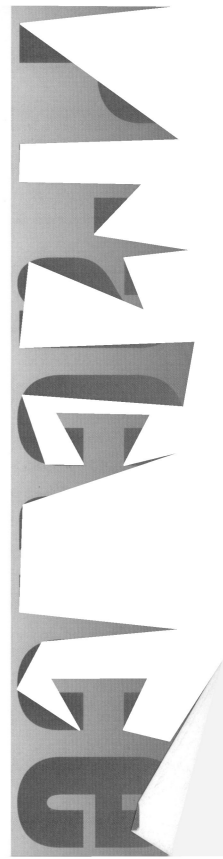

SERIES COMMA

A. Revise each sentence by adding commas where they belong.

Example:

Istanbul is a large beautiful and ancient city.

Istanbul is a large, beautiful, and ancient city.

1. My sister my parents and my grandparents all went to see the palace there.
2. In the palace we saw a throne room a swimming pool and some guest rooms.
3. Our tour guide spoke French German and English.
4. The palace rooms were decorated with stones rugs and jewels.
5. People came long ago from India China and Europe to bring the sultan gifts.
6. We were hot tired and hungry after the tour.
7. At lunch we had lamb grapes and baklava.
8. Then we went to the market, which was busy loud and colorful.
9. The apricots figs and dates all looked delicious.
10. That evening we watched boats barges and ferries glide past the city.

B. Proofread each sentence, and rewrite it correctly. Put commas in the correct places. Take out any commas that do not belong.

Example:

My mother my father and, I were eating dinner.

My mother, my father, and I were eating dinner.

11. We were having lamb chops, mashed potatoes and, peas.

12. Lightning flashed thunder crashed, and rain began falling.

13. The wind, whistled howled and moaned.

14. Thunder rumbled, crashed and boomed.

15. The windows rattled, the screen door banged, and, the lights all went out.

16. Lightning jumped leaped and danced across the, sky.

17. I shivered moaned, and cried.

18. The house, was damp dark and scary.

19. My mother brought out, a flashlight a candle and matches.

20. Mom Dad and, I did not feel like eating.

21. We told jokes played games and sang, songs.

22. The lightning thunder and rain, finally stopped.

23. Then the lights the air conditioner and the radio, came back on.

Note: Italic page numbers in main headings refer to additional practice.